Best wishes
G.L. Farebee

FLESH, SPIRIT, AND STEEL

by

G. L. "Red" Farabee

A Hearthstone Book

Carlton Press, Inc. New York, N.Y.

©1988 by G. L. "Red" Farabee
ALL RIGHTS RESERVED
Manufactured in the United States of America
ISBN 0-8062-3220-X

DEDICATION

This book is dedicated to a family of strong-hearted loved ones who will remember many of these events—the ones who endured many of these hardships that seemed impossible to bear, and never complained. During the years of living in a small twenty-nine foot trailer, moving from place to place our family grew strong spritualy and a bonding love for each other. Our two teenaged daughters and two sons faced the challenges met, as true troopers. They kept their heads and standards high, choosing fine friends and maintaining clean lives. Thanks be to God!

To Louise Bates Farabee, a devoted wife and mother who struggled through some difficult times guiding, caring for and advising her family through the nomad days. As I have said many times, she is the kind of woman who settled the West. Our many times of laughing and rejoicing together are sweet thoughts, even today.

The Farabee troopers were Nicaea Lugenia Farabee, Now Mrs. F. Wayne Overbeek of Holland Michigan; Ivol Lynn Farabee, now Mrs. Richard J. Kloote of Jenison, Michigan; Mr. Ben Garlin Farabee, now with Ford Motor Company in London, England; and Mr. David Alfred Farabee of Holland, Michigan.

We met many great people whose names should be on this page, and the good friends I worked with that gave their lives to this challenging and deadly game never leave this writer's mind.

—G.L. (Red) Farabee

CONTENTS

A Reunion of Steel Erectors	9
From Pride To Humility In One Hour	11
The Headless Horse	16
"The Unknown Shot"	16
The Riveter's Trademark	17
Safety First	18
The Young Psychologist	19
Whirlaway Wins	20
The Nature Man Wins	20
Kentucky's Love	21
Bus To Flint, Michigan	23
A Nervous Man Made More Nervous	23
Lessons In Flint	25
The Diplomat From Birmingham	28
The Tooth Brush Mystery	29
To Atlanta and Bust	30
The Volunteer Fire Fighters	32
Only One To a Box	34
Home Brew Business Sold Out	37
Beyond the Fears at Redstone	38
The Atomic Bomb Job	40
Women	41
Last Union Meeting	43
The Weak and Peace	43
A Rapid Promotion	45
Snap Out and Snap In	47
A Wild Hog Hunt In Louisiana	49
The Alligator Hunt #1	52
The Alligator Hunt #2	55
Fishing In Fear	56
Rigid Rules	58
Streator, Ill	59
Hurricane in Louisiana	61
Unknow Preparation	63
New Orleans	64
To Live Again	67

Hard To Swallow	67
Acid Rain	69
Death Strikes Again	71
Run, Run, Run or Die	73
The Clean and Efficient Power Supply	75
Store Electricity in Homemade Lake	76
Pioneers On Steel	79
Sweet Revenge	80
The La Super Dome	82
Wrong Does Pay	84
Another Sad Day	86
The Impossible Foot Warmer	87
Much Maturing Needed Tobacco Or Red?	88
Another Good Lesson In Detroit	89
Strong Connections	90
The Local 58 Labor Day Float	91
The Wrong Line	94

The Iron Worker's Dictionary

1. gun (pistol)-riveting gun
2. cat head-top piece across strong post to lift from
3. rooster head-top part of crane boom
4. pee whistle-turn to some degree
5. American side-safe
6. Arkansas side-dangerous side
7. lob sided-not balanced
8. stinger-welding lead and rod holder
9. whip-cable for welding
10. horse cock-a buckling bar to drive rivets
11. Old Man-foreman or pusher
12. nine bar-bar used to back up rivets while being driven
13. cata wompus-off center
14. gin mill-bar or saloon
15. whiskey stick-a level
16. guts-plunge in riveting gun
17. cheater-extra leverage
18. foot dragging-lazy
19. Ethiopia language-cussing
20. female trouble-marriage trouble
21. drag-receive money in advance for working
22. drag up-take all personal belongings and leave job site
23. cough up-pay up your obligations
24. headache ball-the weight on cable from hoist to pull cable back to ground from the spool
25. hit the drik-a fall into the river
26. jib-extension of crane boom
27. runner-a fast cable or load from crane jib
28. dead man-a planted cross-tie or railroad tie to be used to pull from at an angle where no other source is available
29. guy-a cable or line used to hold a preferred item at a desired position

A REUNION OF STEEL ERECTORS

The cute little waitress went over to the booth near the corner. She was smiling as she asked this group of men what they wanted for breakfast. The loud talk and sometimes almost vulgar language convinced one these were an unusual breed of workmen sitting here. This loud talking was meant just for this group, but could be heard clear and plain for a city block. When the tall guy put his order in for his breakfast, it was just as if a bomb exploded behind me. "Three cat heads and one slab of a guilt," was a special order for Monroe Sims of New Orleans, L.

Monroe had spent several years booming over the USA working red iron. This is the work of structural steel erectors, the ones that go into the air and wait for the steel to arrive, then assemble the steel beams and columns to make it safe and suitable for normal construction men to work on. Monroe was known through the country as one of the best of the trade. These kinds of people always go in gangs or pairs, seldom do iron workers travel alone. The reason for some of this is that on the job they must work in pairs. It has been the philosophy of many steel erection foremen that one man was not worth his wages and would not hire him or would send him back home until a partner was hired for him. Some of these men would rather go back home than to work with a greenhorn, or rookie, a new man that is unknown to him.

Yes, a man's life is in jeopardy from 8:00 a.m. to 4:30 p.m. when working several floors above the streets on a skeleton of a building. It is so easy to be pushed or forced into the big hole, time eliminates many men; some are crippled for the remainder of their lives, some are killed on the job, some have the jitters and leave the job, some are left ouside, not hired, because others refuse to work with them. Yes, it is important who you work with in steel erection.

Monroe was not only a good man on steel, but a good welder. He could pass the most rigid welding test with old beat up juke box machines. This man would never let up talking. I think he did this to convince himself to be a better workman. Many times I found myself on dangerous jobs singing to myself, or talking to myself, or repeating; my plans over and over step by step. This may sound silly to some, but not to a good journeyman iron worker.

I had just left the Atomic Bomb job in Oakridge, Tennessee. There was an addition to the steel mills in Birmingham that attracted many men throughout the Southland. Virginia Bridge was know through the iron workers as a group of "going Jessies." No man could please the foreman for this company. I have heard them say that a six-foot man reporting to this job at 8:00 a.m. would end the workday at 4:30 p.m. measuring approximately 42"-46" from his nose to the ground. You know this employee was tuckered out at sundown. Gave Virginia Steel all he had.

These so-called slave drivers did not discourage men from coming to Birmingham if they were hungry, when the rent was due, or a car payment to be made. The job steward would meet many hungry Joes at the gate for work. The majority of these men knew of each other from various jobs throughout the country, if not from personal experience. These fellows always met at a favorite bar. Then, if the doors were ever locked, at closing time the steelworkers would always help the bartender lock up. I guess it was because they wanted to find things in good order the next day.

The foreman, men, stewards, and business agents all gathered at a this special bar nearest the job and talked jobs and men. The first question every business agent was asked without fail would be. "Have you got any men loafing? How many?" The next question was, "Have you got any overtime jobs going?"

The business agent is *just that,* he is the agent who takes care of the iron workers business. This includes placing men on a job or removing them from a job. Also, they see that the company does not abuse the union rules against the employees. Some boomers, (traveling iron workers), would arrive in a city with no address, but request the mail be sent to the union hall. This also made a mailman of the business agent. The business agent would always have a list of names of some fellow members that had been broken up, had fallen, on the job someplace, or a list or donations to give to a good friend's widow and children left alone due to a spill into the big hole. This was a normal event that occurred at the least one time a week.

During good times the men get more independent, talk louder and shake their heads in a negative twist with more determination. During bad times when jobs are scarce, the same men go to work under the most adverse conditions. When a rabble rouser is discovered or a tough union man shows up who knows all the rules and regulations, the best policy was to make him a foreman. These men usually made the best foremen for the company. I suppose a person needs a chance to stretch his wings. There is a great desire in man to be a boss.

The first 20 years I found very exciting. Men and jobs were a new challenge constantly. I still find myself, when talking to various groups using the iron workers lingo. I never notice it until I hear chuckles in the crowd. The men who work with you all for many days, sometimes weeks, are never known by their street or home names. It's always a nickname that some intelligent original-minded buddy hangs on these fellow employees. Let me introduce you to some of my good friends. Please meet: Hog Jaw, One Gone, Never Sweat, Bad Eye, Cork-eye, Chicken Neck, Motor Mouth, Cast Arm, East Lake, and many other such titles. Seldom is a man known by his real name.

I hope you by this time will realize that Monroe put his order in for his breakfast for three home-made biscuits and bacon or a piece of salt pork. Monroe knew where most all the iron workers were working, how much time the men were getting, who had been killed or injured. So it was not long until I knew as much as Monroe.

FROM PRIDE TO HUMILITY IN ONE HOUR

Lynchburg, Tennessee

I must back up and tell you when I first met Monroe. As the war clouds began to hover over this nation of ours in 1940, our government leaders began to prepare seriously to protect our shores. We found ourselves very much unprepared for war. We had no powder plants except a few used to make fire crackers, etc. Our ships were not equipped to handle a real war. Planes and guns were not plentiful, and it was becoming clear that if America had to fight a war we had better prepare! So time was important in our good old USA.

I was working in the steel mills when the big rush began. My brother Joe asked me to consider going to a job with him and a few other men at the army camp in Tullahoma, Tennessee. This a large area in a God-forsaken county of south central Tennessee. The name of the camp was "Camp Forest." Our part of the project was to build the boilers and buildings for the laundry and hospital area. I had five years of steel mill experience behind me as a machinist, and this new life for me was exciting, very free and challenging. I could hear them old timers tell of the big money. The iron workers scale in Birmingham, Alabama at that time was 92½¢ per hour. The next union contract hoped to be $1.00 per hour.

As I left the steel mills on a Sunday afternoon, I used that strong point of $1.00 per hour to console my young wife. I closed the gate behind me leaving her behind with our two young girls, one barely walking and the other one too young to even wave good bye. This scene gave the big red-headed construction worker a terrible ache in his heart. But big money was ringing in my ears-and still is forty years later. "Maybe next year I'll get enough ahead to quit this hard, rough game," keeps me driving ahead.

As we drove into the small town of Lynchberg, Tennessee, December 12, 1940, my pockets bulged with eight dollars and sixty cents. I had planned on returning home for the next weekend so that should provide enough money for me. This was my very conservative arithmetic.

Lynchberg had already rolled up the sidewalks at 8:00 p.m. There was no one out, nothing moving except a shadow of a man approximately two blocks away. A place to sleep and eat was badly needed by these two construction men. My brother and I rushed down his way and introduced ourselves. Seems that with our exciting way of talking and convincing manner we interested him enough for a trial run at taking in boarders. That's how the high school professor and his wife began keeping two iron-worker boarders. I know they never forgot those interesting days. Mrs. Jones had majored as a dietition in college, but had never had a chance to put her knowledge into practice. Now she had a chance to demonstrate her ability to feed us as we should be fed.

Monday morning I met Monroe from Mobile, Alabama and what a characters he was. A good worker with vast experience in every field of interest, this man had a whirlpool of answers ready, whether you were ready for them or not. Old construction guys like Monroe would help us eat our lunches day after day without an invitation. Mrs. Jones would pack our lunches as if feeding a logging gang. Many days we would have six to eight sandwiches, plus pies and fruit. These old men on the job told us the first thing to always remember is never take any food back home from work, and never say they packed too much lunch. Say it was always just right. Yes, Joe and I were feeding a complete riveting gang on the job.

I remember this boarding house was directly across the street from the Jack Daniels Distillery in Lynchberg, the only legal distillery in Tennessee. So, many times our first stop from work was, not Jones', but Jack's. The sour corn mash that filled the large wooden vats seemed to be waiting just for us. The big gourd cut out for a big dipper was used so much that the handle was already wore out. The next stop was at the front door of Mrs. Jones, to examine our eyes. I remember she commented one evening after a hard sixteen hours driving rivets on top of a smoke stack in a hard north wind, "You need some 'goose meat. The rivet scales in our eyes were enought to put us in the hospital and, after the trip to Jack Daniels, our red eyes were qualified to be in the town jail. Yes, we two nice-talking borders kept this poor couple terribly confused.

One day the professor invited us to visit the high school. The weather on the smoke stack was entirely too bad for us to work, so it was a perfect day to go to school. Mr. Jones had briefed us on the nice lunches the school provided for only a few cents, so we planned to test them that day. At approximately 10:00 a.m. that morning after a brief visit to Jack Daniels and a slow walk up the hill, we arrived in front of the school building. Our eyes were almost in a state of eclipse. Joe, Monroe and myself met the awaiting professor, and after an introduction to the football coach, we decided to visit science class.

This was a mixed class of boys and girls. The teacher introduced us to the class and told them about our kind of work and opened the discussion for questions. Everyone in the part of Tennessee knew of the job we were doing; the smoke stack could be seen for miles all around. One brilliant young lad had a question I will never forget, or the answer either! The question was, how did we put steel up higher than the other steel, how did we keep going higher and higher setting steel and no crane above? Monroe had that answer on the tip of that heavy, thick tongue. He fumbled and fumbled and could not explain anything. So it was suggested he go to the blackboard and draw a picture of our method of raising the steel.

Up Monroe went to do his drawing, and what a crude drawing he did. As he drew the pole we used and the gate blocks we used, the kids, both girls and boys, began to snigger and chuckle. Monroe was not aware of how it looked from the back of the room. His words were okay, but his drawing would have been comfortable in a sex magazine. I got up and found my way to the blackboard and erased the rigging Monroe had drawn up. We left school very soon after lunch feeling very humble. I recommended that Monroe stay away from school as long as there were kids there, or next time, bypass Jack Daniel's headquarters.

This was a very firm union job. There was no crossing over of craft. Good men were used, and they worked hard to complete the job. One day I was planning to "drag up," quit the job. This would have disrupted the entire crew. On Friday night as we left the job, we wrote inside the smoke stack at the top, "This is a snake job." Did you know there were three different union riveting gangs that came to work there and would leave the job not telling the supervisor why they were leaving? The union men sure did cling together then. We came back to the job after long-distance calls, and finished the job under another agreement.

Our entertainment was a road house approximately four miles up the gravel road, and a rough spot it was, but it seemed that the rougher and tougher spots drew more people. This place was not only operated by, but "manned" by a mean-looking fellow approximately 6' 6" tall and 240 lbs. The place was approximately 12' wide and 60' long, but shot-gun style, long and narrow.

Along the long counter the the bartender had small baseball bats approximately every eight to ten feet apart. He could stand at any place behind the counter and grab a bat and swing it over to klonk anyone on the head across the bar.

This place ran wild until approximately 3.00 Sunday morning. The state troopers would come by and pick up the ones he had knocked out and drag them to the side of the road. I made a remark that anyone could come by there on a beautiful sunny Sunday morning and pick up a syrup bucket of eyeballs. Anyone who attended that place he was afraid to drink and afraid not to drink. I always felt good to get back to the rooming house without Bumps on my head. When the job was completed, each one went his separate way all over the USA. Now you may understand why when two or more iron workers, "steel erectors," meet, there is much to talk about. And the main subject is always: Where is the next big job? Is there any overtime there?

My next job was Louisville, Kentucky, in a large powder plant for E. I. Dupont. This job was unusually large, and once again the places for construction men to live were definitely scarce. I still marvel at how everyone would support the big major objective. Young men left farms, mothers and dads gave up their daughters and sons to wartime defence jobs for this great endeavor. Many would say that only the great desire for money led to this great move. I say a great-test of patriotism arose through out this great land. It proved again that its great people, were willing to sacrifice much for its heritage.

Louisville, Kentucky and Charleston, Indiana

In Louisville, Kentucky proved to have some of the greatest people I have ever met. During these days, my wife, two children, and myself enjoyed many good times together there.

We met old people there that could not work to defend our country; could not contribute anything, or so they thought. Actually they made great sacrifices. Some would go and sleep in a coal pit and let you, "if you were a defense worker," have their bed so you would be more able to perform your daily work. "May God bless them and theirs." I often wonder how America would arise to another all-out war effort today. Maybe as you continue to read this book you will gather my opinion on this as I view it from the viewpoint of a construction worker.

THE HEADLESS HORSE

My wife, two daughters and I landed in a rooming house in the summer of 1941. I was scheduled to report in for the E.I Dupont construction job twenty miles north in Indiana. The cities and states made every effort to favor their large jobs with good roads. Railroad companies provided work trains to get employees to job sites at proper working hours. Sometimes as many as two to five thousand men would ride these work trains. Small sack lunches were available for 50¢ as we loaded up on these trains at 7:00 A.M. Evening time found this tired group of construction workers bumping over the rails in old converted boxcar viewing the countryside, dry throats longing for the first stop at the river in Jeffersonville, Indiana. Where they could swallow some cold beers. Men were saving their energy and breath; there was no wise cracking or small talk, just quiet riding except for the clattering rails. I was sitting where I could view the coutryside. I had ridden this train ten times a week for weeks. I knew every flower along the way, as did all the men riding this train.

I saw a big burley red-headed man jump up after passing only a cow and calf in a pasture and yell, "That ain't no suds mill (beer joint)!" That statement drew more attention than anything that could have been said. Every man on this work train looked out and the realization of what was happening came like a shot. We were riding a headless horse! We had been uncoupled from our engine and left free riding through the country on our own. We all knew this was a dangerous situation to be in. Someone had thrown a switch, or something had happened that sure displeased this group of construction workers. But luckily in a short time we were riding on the right rails into Louisville. After a few beers, all this was forgotten.

"THE UNKNOWN SHOT"

A few days later as we were riding the same train to Louisville, another exiting event happened that drew a FBI investigation.

Seems as if everyone on the train was sleeping. These construction jobs and their locations made long and tiring days. Very faithful newspaper boys would meet us at every gate to give us a chance to learn the latest news of the war's progress. Us tired men's schedule was to get a paper, glance at the latest happenings, and load up on the train to sleep until the different sound of clattering rails woke us up. As we crossed the Ohio River, the wheels made a different sound on the railroad tracks. This was the arousing signal.

On this particular day, everyone had just gone to sleep. I heard a loud shot near my head; glass flew across the car. My ear was filled with glass. Luckily I had my eyes shut. As I brushed the glass from my face and ears, I was cut up badly. The blood ran down my face, neck, and clothes. Several of the workmen got glass in their eyes. Yes, the FBI met us in Louisville for questioning and medical attention. Some men thought this was a sabotage job, but nothing proved this to be true. Probably some teenage boys out in the Indiana farm were trying out their new guns or playing war. But this could have ended in a very tragic event.

THE RIVETER'S TRADEMARK

Very few construction men are not aware of how safety-minded and employer E.I. Dupont is. My first experience with them was in Charleston, Indiana on construction of a powder plant. I had driven approximately twenty-five miles to report to work. The job I had just left was a rough, tough riveting job at Tullahoma, Tennessee. "Yes, those hot rivets will burn you." When one is hit or grazed by a hot rivet, he bleeds freely and it always leaves a scar. The scales from a hot rivet while driving it or bucking it will burn and sear and make bad sores all over the body. I had never really healed up from the Tullahoma job when I took the physical exam for the Charleston job.

The doctor noticed a big red streak down my chest, across my stomach, and down on my privates with a few stops along the way where blisters rose. This young doctor was sure he had found a victim of a very bad and dangerous venereal disease. He called his doctor friend over to give a special examination to my penis. I assured this man that all was well with me; that I had a good penis, and in just a day or two it would be healed again.

This hot rivet scale was giving me more trouble that just pain.

I was to stay in Louisville, Kentucky until I healed up. I could imagine the added expense to me. The food, room, and other expenses with no income. These thoughts encouraged me to plead with these two young doctors like and evangelist calling for converts. After a few minutes of super persuasive power, I could feel I was winning. The agreement was that I would go to work now and report back to them the following Monday and let them look me over. Well, the job was so interesting and busy, and so many other things came up that when Monday morning rolled around I didn't have time to go back to the doctors'. Monday evening passed so fast I didn't see my good doctor friends. But Tuesday morning here came the patrol and doctors looking for their victim. "Yes, a *private* examination was held" the embarassment was doubly increased when I saw the woman in the front seat with my doctor friend. I learned two good lessons from this incident. Or should I say three.

SAFETY FIRST

This job in Charleston, Indiana provided many profitable experiences for me. I will always remember the time a crane boom got tangled up in some unusually hot electric wires. This happened at approximately 2:00 p.m. In a quick flash, five men lay on the ground in an area of approximately eighty feet. Not a groan or quiver came from any of them. A large hot wire was crackling and bouncing over the area. It was unusual for something like this to happen to this company's employees. E.I. Dupont was rated #1 for talking, preaching, and practicing safety on the job. Some even labeled them very radical. Yes, I did until I saw this happen and how they handled this terrible accident. As soon as this happened, I saw five safety men who took complete control of the operation. The area was cleared from further danger from high-powered lines and no man was moved, but artificial respiration began on the spot where they lay.

Dark clouds were moving in from the west and it began to look as if all was going to be drowned in a few minutes. I wondered what they would do with their patients. I thought maybe they would drag them to a nearby building and complete their treatment, but no, the safety men of E.I. Dupont began to give orders to carpenters and within a few minutes a building was constructed over each man just where he lay. A trench was dug to funnel the rain water away. The artificial respiration continued without missing a stroke.

The amazing conclusion was that three of the men were brought back to life! As I watched this I thought about wives and children waiting for these men to come home that evening, and the importance of safety and proper care of patients was sure multiplied to me. It seems no matter how hard the company and its employees try to prevent accidents, some will happen. No, we have not reached the stage where we do not have some accidents today, but not as many as in previous years.

Several years ago, the contractor would figure in his bid for jobs that for every one million dollars, he would have to pay for one man to be killed. On ten million dollar job it seemed as if ten men must die. Construction safety began to change during the war years.

THE YOUNG PSYCHOLOGIST

We had completed some of the buildings, enough to install tanks, piping, etc. Everyone was busy getting his part of the job ready for operation. I was walking through a building at approximately 2:00 p.m. when a foreman from St. Louis asked me to help him move a safeway scaffold. This scaffold had him jammed so close to his desk that he could not write out his daily time cards. The pipe fitter had just left the rolling scaffold and all the materials to be used still lay on top of it. The pipe fitter planned to return soon and continue hanging the pipe throughout the building.

Well, Mr. Carlton needed more room and I was to help him push the scaffold away. I had learned enough to pull the scaffold and have Carlton push. This foreman was wearing a large leather cap with a big button in the top. Well, as we moved the scaffold, a hanger above dragged a loose valve from above and it landed on top of the foreman's head knocking him out cold. He and I were the only ones in that area. His cap was lying to one side and a four-inch brass valve weighing approximately twenty pounds was lying directly in front of Mr. Carlton.

I helped this poor man to his knees. He was stunned, and in great pain he asked me, "What hit me, Red?"

I had to answer and I didn't want to excite him too much. I reviewed all my psychology I had learned and decided to use these words. "Mr. Carlton, all that hit you was that little ole valve lying there." He slowly turned his head and looked it over and dropped out again just like a light. He came back to consciousness late that night. Now it's imperative that all construction personnel must wear hard hats on job sites. That would have eliminated this injury.

When a time for layoff came, a check was made on your automobile in the parking lot. If you had ragged, beat-up fenders on your vehicle, you were sure to receive a layoff. "Unsafe on the road, unsafe on the job."

WHIRLAWAY WINS

While we were in Louisville, Churchill downs produced one of the world's most treasured champions. Whirlaway was the undisputed champion in 1941. I learned to appreciate the work, time, and money spent to develop a champion, plus the expensive chances that are taken through breeding and training. As I look at a racehorse now, I look for certain features and actions of this animal. Some good horseflesh never develops into a good racing horse due to some trivial factor, probably through breeding, early fears, or training care. It's a great privilege to be in Louisville, Kentucky during April and May of any year. All hotel rooms are filled and the streets are jammed with people loaded with the well known Kentucky bourbon.

THE NATURE MAN WINS

A very strange event happened while we were in Louisville, Kentucky. As a local doctor was traveling from the southeast part of the state, he located a man lying in the road. He gathered the old fellow up and brought him into the hospital in Louisville. He was treated and gained his health and strength back in a few hours. But the strange part was he escaped and left no trails at all. No name, no address, no nothing of this wild man who went back to the hills for another eighty years to live. I Think he was super wise because his life could have easily been shortened in this city. If he were not run down by the traffic, the drink would kill him. Kentucky is not this kind of state now. It is a beautiful and prosperous section of the U.S. with beautiful cattle, great farms, barns and white fences that ribbon the country for miles and miles. The tobacco fields and barns spell out to be much money.

Any lover of nature would truly love this state. It has so much to offer that only Kentucky has: beautiful caves under the mountains, trees and flowers of all kinds growing wild in their natural habitat. There is nuch here to be enjoyed.

KENTUCKY'S LOVE

Every construction worker knew there were plans to build the world's largest powder plant somewhere north of Louisville, Kentucky. By the time I arrived the bulldozers had began clearing out trees and brushes, and anyone could see that big things were going to happen there.

On my first trip to Louisville, Kentucky the people made me feel as this had been my home for many years. I checked out the job site across the Ohio river at the small town of Charleston, Indiana. The woods and farmland provided much needed space for this type of manufaturing. The water was plentiful from the near by river. This was a perfect place for the world's largest powder and T. & T. plant to be built.

The labor force could be drawn from southern Ind. and throughout Kentucky. The shipping of the finished products could be trucked four ways and a good railroad system was readily available. The Ohio River provided a perfect water way out. The selection of this area proved to be a wise one. One that would employ approximately 120,000 workers.

My decision was to live in Louisville while I was on the powder plant job. I located a room at the Brizella Boarding House on Third Street. The people were so gracious to me, both the young and the old. They made me realize that there were still many good people around, even in northern Kentucky.

Some of our closest friends of even today began there around the long dining table in this Kentucky home. There we met two young girls, that was a great help to us. Louise and I were struggling with two small children in a strange city. Juanita and Sarabeth were our answered prayer. Every evening the stroller trip led to various places of interest. They were of great help to us. Our friendship has continued to be close even sicne 1941. We still visit each other and share some of the old Third Street stories.

I remember when Louise first came to Louisville riding a big train up from Alabama. The steam engine was like a big monster standing there smoking a black smoke that wraped a black blanket over the entire area. White shirts turned black. Suitcases were covered with that black coal dust. The small white girls were now black girls.

Our group collected together to part for the boarding house, but the large monsters let our a loud frightening noise that shook the entire earth, it was signal that it was leaving town. Well that didn't bother us as much as that Nicaea our oldest daughter began to leave too. After running her down and checking her out my heart beat was about 350 per minute. She has never forgotten some of those old train rides.

There has been much moving and address changing since the night we met around the large dining table loaded with super food. There I noticed that you don't have to be grumpy when you get older. The elders there both men and women were great fun to be with. Our experiences at the Brizella Boarding House were rewarding to us.

When visiting with Bill and Juanita the conversation leads to far out Japan, Turkey, a North Pole, atomic bombs, Korea, etc. but they always return to northern Kentucky. In fact that is where this couple came to retire. The drawing power of these great people cannot be tossed aside lightly.

Bill and Juanita bought an old colonial home in Glasgow, Kentucky to repair and fix for their retirement. When we visited there in the spring of 1986, I had no trouble locating their home. Remember Bill is a transplanted Yankee. His home address is 500 Cleveland Street, and I believe he had the largest, brightest American flag that he could find flying in the breeze off his front porch. I thought how far he had come since leaving New York

City as a young man. I think he was singing "my old Kentucky home" while rocking at full tilt in the old Abe Lincoln rocking chair. That Bill converted into a true Kentuckian.

BUS TO FLINT, MICHIGAN

Flint, Michigan

My friend and I left Panama City not knowing where we were going, but on arrival in Birmingham, our next job was settled. Our B.A. knew in Flint, Michigan, the American Bridge & Iron Co. was changing all the old wood structures to steel for Buick. This job was designed and planned to be changed to a new and modern plant, without stopping production of those new Buick cars. Safety was not the first word in the American Bridge book at that time. Most steel erectors shunned this company saying they were too rough; their foremen and superintendents were hard and mean. They had a reputation for killing too many men. This created a challenge for a young iron worker, and opportunity to meet new men and methods of building boiled in my blood.

A NERVOUS MAN MADE MORE NERVOUS

I met an old-timer in Birmingham who wanted to go with me to Detroit to this Buick Job. Floyd was well known throughout the bridgemen world. He was a good riveter and fit in any part of a riveting gang. Heater, catcher, bucker, he could do any of these. Floyd and I loaded up on a Greyhound bus with the Detroit sign infront. Two days and three nights later, we were visiting the union hall.

The business agent there was of Italian descent and sure was doing a good job for local#25. As usual, a boomer gets the worst job in the locality. These jobs can be accepted or rejected, but as hungry as we were, all we thought of was accepting the job in Flint with American Bridge. This was a cold, black day; it seemed as we would never see the sun again. I shivered and shook in my icecream pants. I left Florida without even a pair of long-handle underwear. We got our permit from the business agent to travel north to Flint and report in to the superintendent on

the job the next morning. Floyd was an unusually good buddy to travel with, easy to please, never grumbleing about food or conditions. He came from a family that had produced five brothers known over the US as the best iron workers that had ever climbed a column. Many years at this work soon has an effect on a guy's complete life. He becomes nervous, and he wants action now. But things don't always fall together as we would like. So I must say Floyd was a very nervous and easily excited man.

We checked back to the bus station in Detroit to get our suitcases and to transfer to Flint. I handed over my ticket for my baggage, but poor Floyd could not find his ticket. He became so excited he could not even identify it; not the color or anything about it. Finally after a long pleading conversation with the baggage man, we decided on the certain suitcase that had the rope around it. This "Oh, please don't rain" suitcase looked as it had boomed over the US roads and railways. Someone had sure got good mileage out of it and it showed it. The baggage man said he would let us open it if we could describe the contents. Yes, Floyd says, "My belt and tools are right on top and some bull pins in the handkerchief bins." So open came that suitcase and would you believe that women's clothes were all we could find in that bag. Boy did I feel little. I thought Floyd was going to cry and fall over. I expected the baggage man to kick us out of there, "But I said, "I was never sure that was the right suit case. The right one was "over there" and I pointed it out. We opened it and, sure enough, it was. The iron workers belt was right on top. Were there two happy men ready to head north to Flint! We had just settled down and relaxed when Floyd reached for a cigarette and pulled out a baggage check for that troublesome baggage.

LESSON IN FLINT

The next morning we checked in and were written up for the job. We received our pep talk and headed to the top of the four-story structure. As we climbed the long shaky ladder outside the building, we met three gangs of men dragging up. "Too damn cold," they said.

It might have been too cold for them, but for this Alabama

boy's vote, he voted *nay*. The major factor in this decision was the very thin pocket book, and the $2.25 per hour paid to us to make it to the top. There were two stiff leg derricks erected on top of the old building to handle steel over the production areas below. I was assigned to help move the derrick down the building, approximately two hundred feet.

The cold, whistling wind off Lake Huron was soon forgotten when a large 16" x 16" x 30' timber rolled over and caught my big toe on my right foot. I was so thankful it was cold, the pain was just numb. I could feel blood in the shoe, but was afraid to pull it off for two reasons. I knew if the foreman saw it I wouldn't get to work anymore, and the second reason was I would doubt ever getting my shoe back on again. That day at noon more men left the job, "drug up", too cold, work too rough, and that "fog Horn" of a man we were working for was too unbearable. "They say it's impossible to please that so and so." "We should push him off the building." I told Floyd I had to last out the day to get my bus fare into town, and tomorrow we would make another decision.

That afternoon as we left the job, I was sore, hurting, cold, and hungry, but on the way to my hotel room, I stopped and bought a large box of Epson salts and a Detroit Free Press newspaper. As soon as I took my bath I began to soak my busted toe in hot water and Epsom salts. I read *every* word in the newspaper as my toe soaked. The next morning, it was in a "go" condition.

I began to enjoy the job. My pusher was a tough old man, but he definitely knew the game and men. At that time the foreman selected qualified men with the purpose in mind to get the job done now, and well. Seems that this policy has changed and today's foreman adjusts to his men's personalities and tries to be winner of a popularity contest. Foremen today are fired because the men under them do not like them regardless of their knowledge and experience and qualifications. As I learned to like and respect ole Fog Horn, we became good friends.

This building ran approximately twelve-hundred feet alongside of a highway. It was designed just right for two raising gangs to work under exactly the same situations side by side. American Bridge had just completed a job in up-state New York and had a lot of Indians on their payroll. They had crossed the Canadian border at Buffalo, New York. Many of these followed American

Bridge to their next job at Flint. So we had one gang of Indians and one gang of Americans racing side by side.

Yes, this proved very interesting, but it seemed to me the Indians had more accidents and more injuries due to carelessness. I do believe the Indians would manuever better on high steel, but when they arrived to the point of work, they didn't know how to take advantage of particular jobs. Too many were mashed or knocked off of buildings for not clear thinking. They were a special people and some good tough bridgemen came out of Buffalo area. I know of several good riveters that could sure take the heat and hard work. I enjoyed working with them until the whistle blew for quitting time. The first stop, "a bar." Then trouble continued on until daylight. If the bartender refused to serve them liquor, there was much more trouble. Where most Americans will *talk* off a drunk, they would have to *fight* it off with some one.

The Reed brothers from Nashville were on the job there during the erection of the steel. These were good bridgemen known all over to be the best in the game. One of the brothers was pushing the riveting gang there. One day, while dropping by to chat with a gang driving rivets over a crane runway, Walter wanted to drive a few rivets to relieve one of the gang. Well, the scaffold they were driving from fell and Walter fell approximately thirty-five feet below on to concrete, breaking both arms. This was a sad situation for him and his wife, they were trying to move luggage from hotel to hotel with two small children in their arms. Both arms in a sling trying to heal, and two young children just able to stand alone and four large suitcases. During the war, the rules were construction workers could stay only two nights in a hotel. This was a regular moving deal, across town every other day. Not only he and his wife and children were glad when Walter healed up but his whole gang was happy.

This job was quite an experience to me; the large cranes were not conceivable. When a large load of steel would come in, the big crane would swing around and get the complete load of steel and set it far off out of our way. Forty and fifty tons of steel were like handling an arm full of stove wood. There was nothing to it. American Bridge had good men and good tools to work with. When big jobs are to be built, American Bridge is always ready to do them. They knew where to put a finger on the best riveters in America. Big steel jobs did not alarm this American Bridge Company.

THE DIPLOMAT FROM BIRMINGHAM

On a trip looking for a job, I landed in Detroit approximately at 11:00 p.m. on a dreary cold and rainy night. On this particular expedition I was alone. I was hoping things would work out; that the next day I would be on some company's steel job; but until then, I was in search of a cheap but clean hotel. If you know Detroit, you can find hotels as cheap as any place. Well, I found one about as cheap as I thought I could stand. Since this was done, I felt as I should not venture too far from my room or my home base, so I turned the corner and into a bar; I sneaked over near the wall into a booth and placed my order. I knew I was in a lively spot. The loud talk and demands and strong language were increasing by the minute. It appeared that this one man dominating the floor was winding the event up for a big showdown and very soon.

I felt fairly safe over near the wall where I could not be noticed. After finishing my meal I eased up to the cash register to pay and get out of that hot spot before it blew and I got hurt. This daring, brave man that had several big guys around him stood off to one side noticed me, and recognized me as an old steel erecting buddy. I weighed approximately two hundred pounds and looked as if I was in good physical condition. Well, Cast Iron Jones of Cairo, Illinois greeted me with a big, "Come and help me!" I could not start running, as bad as I wanted to. I knew I had nothing to fight about there, so I converted all my fighting skill into a peacemaker. Cast Iron kept telling them how I could, and would whip them all. Well, I had a good visit there with Cast Iron. The last time we were together was in Chicago. There was much to talk about. Such as how Jones had never been still long enough to think money and family. His home was in southern Illinois with his mother.

Cast Iron was rugged, rough-talking steel worker that had never refused a drink of liquor, beer, or anything of alcoholic. Sometimes even the job never checked his drinking. Well, after a few minutes of lots of thinking and placing good words at the right place, we walked out of that bar unharmed.

I have always felt that if our national diplomats were as much in earnest to prevent trouble as I was that night, we would never, be in any wars.

I left Cario sitting in front of a church building crying like a baby, this forty-four year old Cario Jones was wanting to go home to see his mother.

THE TOOTH BRUSH MYSTERY

The union halls for iron workers are the most interesting place to visit. The boomers, the drunks, the old toughs, and the young toughs all trying to stress their qualifications of being a real tough he-man, "a bridgemen." Some of the stories and tales in these union halls keep a large audience on their toes with eager ears.

Some of these men are looking for work and some are healing up from job injuries, some come there to play poker for a while and listen to the bull. Once I was in Detroit at Local 25 for approximately four days looking for a steel erection job there. I was not doing much good because too many of their local men were out of work. I was promised a job at the Cadillac plant and was very patiently waiting for it. One day, as I sat waiting, an old acquaintance came in from northern Michigan. Any one that knows Terry knows that he is always loaded to talk and tell tales, or fight, or anything—he is ready. Very few men can hold claim to whipping Terrible Terry. He was a gifted talker and the subjects he was an authority on were unlimited. Some nights out he would be dressed and talking only medical terms. He would be in personating a doctor, a big surgeon. The following night after a day on steel he would be a lawyer. The conversation that night at the bars would all be in legal terms.

Terry had just arrived in Detroit from upper Michigan from a good overtime job. He told me about his roommate up there. He says one day a young man came there from someplace in Texas. Terry, being a good friend to a boomer, promised the new man he could come and room with him until he got straightened our financially, or "until he got a pay day." Their working schedules were not the same. The Texan would get to the room approximately a half hour before Terry. The second evening when Terry came home he found his toothbrush wet. This could make any one wonder about his room mate, and it worried Terry, but this subject was too sensitive to be discussed. Out the next evening Terry found his toothbrush *wet* again.

This kept Terry awake most all night planning his strategy to handle this difficult situation. The next day, Terrible Terry came home a half hour ahead of Tex. When Tex opnened the door and entered, he could see nothing but terrible Terry sitting flat in the middle of the floor rubbing the toothbrush between his toes fast and furious like a wild man. Well, the man from Texas packed up and left and never discussed his reason for leaving, toothbrushes, or bed, or what.

Terry was planning to go to Louisville to check on someone of something. There is something about this iron worker boomers that makes life more interesting and exciting. When a grop of drunken iron workers band together in a fight, someone is sure to get hurt. This trademark has somewhat faded from the craft today. I know the police dapartments are very grateful for this. Terrible Terry left Detroit for Louisville and I left to the construction job in the Cadillac plant.

TO ATLANTA AND BUST

Atlanta
Things got rough for work around Birmingham for steel workers and there was nothing else to do but to boom out. I had never worked in Atlanta before. I suppose one reason was the scale was about twenty-five cents per hour less than the other locals in the South. I checked into the local, and the business agents sent me to the Bell Telephone building downtown. We were erecting nine more floors on top of thirteen stories. The traffic in the streets never stopped at all. Loads of steel would swing over the street filled with cars, buses, and people all day. The city rules, "laws," seemed very weak and dangerous to me. I found out why so few boomers came to Atlanta.

The business agent was also an FBI man and when the local had more jobs than men, he would go borrow some from the prison in Atlanta: some good guys ready for parole or short timers. These fellows didn't know very much, but sure tried to be good and work hard. This would lighten the load for the journeymen. I don't know any kick back was there. We sure worked with some tough guys.

The Winecroff Hotel fire that swept through eight floors of the most elite hotel in Atlanta was a tragedy never to be forgotten. This fire left one hundred-eight dead. The awnings across the street from the hotel were torn up from people jumping out of the burning building to escape. The awning braces that supported the covers were decorated with pieces of human flesh ripped from the bodies of people that had jumped. The blood and water ran down Peach Tree Street for three days and nights after this shocking event. This was truly a sad time for Atlanta and the surrounding area. The state safety board began to make an extensive check on fire escapes and methods to escape from dangers within public buildings. It was stunning to learn that the largest theater in the South did not have fire escapes. Then rigid laws began to be passed and much construction for iron workers began. Overtime was plentiful to all whon wanted to work.

On the last day of 1946 in Atlanta, I fell approximately forty feet. This has long lived with me; I begin to throb on my right side just thinking about it.

I had just been sent to Atlanta Steel Erectors. On my first day with this company, we were in downtown Atlanta. Our first job was changing a large overhead door behind Davis and Paxon department store. The foreman sent me up to take the nuts off the right-end bracket that supported a 40' x 40' roll-up door. Being a new man, I wanted to make good with him, so right up there I went and took all nuts off the bolts except one. I came down preparing to release tension in a large coil spring within the pipe over the door area. Tension was to be released by adjusting rods. Swede saw me and asked me if I had all the nuts off. I reported, all but one, chief. He said, "What in the hell is wrong with that one?" I said there was big spring in that big pipe tuned to the key of G. It was so damn tight and some tension should be eased before removing the last nut. Swede said, "Are you going to take that nut off, or must I get someone else to do it?" I was disgusted and angry and wanted to prove a point to my "intelligent" foreman. I said to Swede, "Come here and watch this," and I led him out away from the building and requested that he watch this. I went back up and removed the last nut from a large bracket. Then it happened. Off it shot. I grabbed a piece of steel that weighed approximately four-hundred pounds and over into a pile of cardboard boxes we both landed, a good distance from where we started. Here comes Swede running over and asking me if it hurt me. I looked up at him and said, "Hell, yes it hurt." The next "intelligent" statement was, "Can you walk on it?" I said to him, "I don't know, but I'll give it a good try." But I didn't do very well at it.

Swede used the next three hours whittling our peg legs and pieces of crates to make me a leg I could use to help me walk. Finally, after such swelling from hip to toe on my right side, I told Swede, "Please forget those peg legs and go in to the parking lot and drive my black Ford car up there where I can get into it, and forget about me." I didn't want him to do anything else for me. Well, he did, only drove in and it was my problem again to back out into the heavy traffic in downtown Atlanta and a bad crippled leg.

I drove back to my hotel room and found my iron worker friend standing in front. I called to him and we located a doctor that refused to do anything to my leg. I was swollen too much. He gave me a pair of crutches and told me to come back when the swelling went down. I drove one hundred twenty miles home that night. Yes, I spent several weeks in a bathtub of hot water. That was like a day's work everyday. I got no insurance, no benefits, and no money. Many things passed through my mind during these days. I suppose revenge was the number one in my thoughts.

THE VOLUNTEER FIRE FIGHTERS

Panama City, Florida

During those first months of World War II, the German subs sure played havoc with our ships. It seemed as if the United States lost a large percentage of boats and cargo to the watery grave in the Atlantic Ocean. The important supplies were much needed for our troops in Europe and Africa. The merchant marines were drawing triple pay to ride our loaded vessels with gun, shells, food, etc. for our soldiers.

The navy began to send the ships out of our harbors and form a convoy a few miles from the American shores. Then large Navy ships would try and protect the cargo from our enemy nesting to destroy. The German military leaders never knew how hard it was to get the American young men to go aboard the cargo carriers. If they had realized the fear that was haunting our coastlines, I do believe our coast would have witnessed some kind of invasion or bombing.

The car lights on our Florida coast were dimmed or blacked out, street lights and unnecessary lights were not used. Anything pertaining to construction jobs and new materials or products were not to be discussed, except in proper places.

I was working in Panama City, Florida on an addition to the paper mill. At evening, the long beach and bars were visited regularly. I made acquaintance with some boys that were in the Air Force from Tyndall Field. Those men would fly planes that pulled a tow target for a group of those red-necked farm boys to shoot at. This is about the most exciting way I can think of to make a pay check. I always felt that a poor steel worker lived a shorter life than anyone else, but these fellows from Tyndall Field didn't seem to last very long either. I can understand why they spent so much of their check for liquor. I can also see why the bars were giving them a bargain for what they drank. When we met after our day of work everything under the sun was discussed except our jobs. I sure learned to appreciate our brave young American servicemen. May God keep them forever in our memories.

One hot night as I lay in my room at the Park Hotel, I looked above the window and noticed a large eye bolt hanging down. This bothered me. Why was it there? A few nights later I found a large coil of 3/4" rope coiled neatly under my bed. My first thought was that another iron worker had been there before me and had stolen more rope than he could travel with and left it there hidden under the bed. Then the connection came to me. This was the early American fire escape. To prepare for service, you just tied one end of rope in the eye bolt and swing down three floors to the ground below. The major drawback to this method was that there was no way to swing away from the power and telephone lines just below the window.

Several days passed and I was reminded of the fire escape when some drunk on the second floor accidentally set fire to his mattress. Smoke filled the second and third floors of the Park Hotel. My roommate and I ran downstairs to his room and managed to get the mattress into the bathtub. The drunk was next in line for the cold water.

Panama City was attractive to all types of people. Some were after easy money, some were patriotic to our nation's call. Some came after the lust for sin. Yes, most all of these characters go together in boom towns. I was blessed to meet, and talk nightly with the author of *"China Town"* in Panama city. Lemennel Debray was a very interesting man to listen to and talk with. He loved this country and was willing to spend many weeks there working in the shipyard. This man inspired me to write. The stories we passed from one to another still travel on to new and hungry ears.

As usual, our construction days in Panama City were ended as abruptly as that began. We never had time to plan a nice exit or bid farewell to everyone we would have liked to. However many good memories of many good people will never be forgotten.

ONLY ONE TO A BOX

Gadsden, Alabama

The Goodyear Tire co. at Gadsden was desperately in need of a big addition to be able to make more tires for trucks, tractors, and passenger cars. The tubes were badly needed for the same. Every steel worker in the eastern United States had his eyes on this job. When is the good year job going to break? Good men were rejecting jobs in order to be ready for the big job.

Well, it finally started. There was a very rough and tough contractor who got the bid to go on the steel erection. Everyone shook and shuddered when Virginia Steel began to make plans to go. They sent a large, tough superintendent in from a Houston, Texas job. When Walter Beck's name was mentioned, some steel workers knew there was no hope for them to work on that job. When Mr. Beck was talking to his personnel, he would act so humble and speak so firm and plain that no one could ever, ever answer back. Positively there was not arguments with this Texan.

One beautiful morning as the men were standing looking at

the steel being set for building, planning their strattegy for the morning, a new man walked up. A very good sized man of approximately 6' 2", weighing about 180 lbs. I looked him over and admired his size and build. The new man began to pull out of a big paper bag new overalls, new shirt, new shoes, I thought, "There is a man of means, an iron worker that made only the best jobs." Mr. Beck was watching his every move, the way he tied those new shoes, how his overall suspenders were handled differently from others, how his hat was cocked on the side of his head. Yes he was the center of attraction on this day.

There were no ladders allowed on steel jobs at that time. If you could not climb those columns, you could not get up there. And if you couldn't get up there, you were of no use then. You were in the wrong place and had to go home. I called this man Toledo because he had mentioned something that happened in Ohio. When someone blew whistle at 8:00 a.m., everyone started climbing columns. Poor Toledo's new clothes and shoes made trouble for him. Walter walked up to Toledo and very quietly suggested to him that he had better run along home to his mama. He would put his hand behind his right ear and say, "I believe I hear your Mama calling you. Run along home, sonny. We have work to do here and youse may get hurt." This was as bad statement that could be made to a steel worker. Well, Toledo changed his clothes and left town. I never heard of his whereabouts anymore.

The turnover of personnel on steel jobs had never been surpassed by another craft. Sometimes the surpervision causes a lot of this and maybe the type job, if dangerous or bad wrecks or accidents happen on the job, men will not come to it. So it's an hour by hour deal even today on steel construction jobs.

One day the crane used for setting steel broke down and needed minor repairs and would not be available for a few hours. This called for a decision for the supervisor. No one would let five men sit for hours waiting until a sick crane healed up. As the foreman says, "That's killing me." so there must be some activity going on even if it's not paying off.

Well, this decision was Beck's today and he glanced down by the railroad tracks and told us to go get that pile of cross ties and bring them up here. We knew as well as Walter did that he didn't need those ties up here, and we would surely have to carry them back if time permitted. If you know what I know about ties, you would shy around them if possible. They weigh approximately 300 lbs. and are full of a heavy, sticky, hot tar. If this tar touched you, you would have a bad burn. There was a big mud hole between the pile of cross ties and here. So off we started the long way around. We began to get cross sticks so the weight of ties could be distributed four ways, and we would keep that tar off us and our clothes. Sure, Beck knew well what we were doing, but he did not approve at all. He came running down to us and shouted that that was no way to carry ties. He grabbed a tie, put it on his shoulder and through the mud hole he went and said "Carry ties like this. One man, and one tie." This looked easy, for Walter he was approximately 230 lbs. of good man, but for my 122 lb. partner, Marvin, it was the impossible. Marvin or so he came up to me and said he was dragging up from the job. That meant he was gathering all his personal belongings and leaving the job for good.

Marvin Walked up to Walter. This scene looked like David and Goliath of the Bible times. Marvin said "I want all my money, Mr. Beck." Mr. Beck: "Why do you want your money, buddy?" Marvin: "I can't carry those damn ties." Mr. Beck: "Why can't you carry those ties, my good man?" Marvin: "Hell, I'm not big enough to carry them" Mr. Beck: "Oh, I can't help it because you're little. You mama had two tits just like mine did. I'll get your money." And Marvin left the job.

Walter was no public relations man , but he sure knew how to communicate to the steel workers.

The men would come in town from all over these United States; some would not even have a belt or tools of any kind. They sold them to get booze or to get out of jail for some common steel worker's problem (alimony). It always amazed me how some people could be such good journeymen and never have any tools or even enough money to eat breakfast. They would always persuade the company to give them a "drag" or advanced pay even before they had earned any. But the supervision knew this kind of man had built the roughest and most dangerous job in America.

When we had completed the structural steel and it was riveted up, the majority of the men left town for other jobs. I stayed in town and just changed contractors. The gang of men was to install a large lamp-black system. This material is very valuable in the manufacture of rubber. This system was to be erected on top of a three-story building. The large tank on top would hold six railroad cars of lamp black plus the many conveyors to transfer the material.

The location of the large tank on top of the building was impossible to reach with cranes, so the hard way was used . As we would say, "We will do it just like they do in the old country."

The hand crab was used to hoist the materials. The materials were unloaded approximately one hundred yards down a railroad track. This procedure called for anchoring the hoist on top of the building at a selected place, then used to drag the large sheets down the railroad track to the building. Then we built on an A-frame on the end of the building to hoist the material to the roof up three floors, where it was to be dragged two-hundred feet down on top of the building to the location for erection. I proved to be the dumbest man on the job. I was the operator on the hand-crab. Needless to say, my job was imperative every minute, day after day no one could wind up the steel but "Bugger Red." A perfect job for physical development, but very bad on the ego.

When the actual erection began, we used a large wooden gin pole up the center in a basket cradle. This was convenient to jump up or move up as the tank building progressed. Well, one day, "it" happened. The pole broke and men started falling to the bottom and on the roof below. My location at the hand-crab post saved me. Men lost hands, fingers, and sustained various kinds of injuries. So every man on the job "drug up" but me. I stayed to finish the job. See, sometimes the journeyman must be his own safety man and if things don't look good to him, he keeps walking and will not work on some jobs.

HOME BREW BUSINESS SOLD OUT

We had established a home there in Gadsden, Alabama, enjoying watching our two girls grow. We lived on a very busy street where the city's large hospital was located. I could sit on the front porch and watch the traffic going to and from the hospital. One summer between contruction jobs, I felt the urge to make a five-gallon churn of home brew, drink known to most in that area. Of course, it was not legal to make. But legal or not every construction guy knew how to make homebrew. Some said put raisins in it to give it more kick. Some said put potatoes in it to give some good headaches, but I went all the way. I used all the ingredients I had ever heard of: yeast, malt, sugar, raisins, potatoes, warmwater, and five days of good quiet rest. This made a most potent drink, cheap to make, but powerful!

I was making regular trips to the chicken house in the backyard. My wife had informed me that *it* or *her* or *me* was definitely slated to go. So the homebrew moved from the chickens house.

A suden call to another job changed my plans and drinking habits. I knew I could not trust the remaining brew in the care of my wife. She was a nervous wreck by now. This was an environment she had never lived in and was not going to live in. To get rid of the brew, I kept close tabs on the traffic walking on Third Street. Every construction worker passing on foot was called by for a good sample of my rukus juice. Black or white. There was no difference after the first drink. So straight to the chicken house we had a trail beat out.

The many visitors going to the hospital were sure in a good mood by the time they reached the bedside of the patients. I remember the loud thanks to me as they would go stumbling out of our yard.

This manner of living lasted about a week and I still had some of that wild juice. Finally, my good neighbor received the remaining two gallons left. When I had enlightened her that she could drink a glass a day and put on some weight, the homebrew was transferred from chicken house to my neighbors house. This was the first night's sleep my wife had had in three weeks. I had made many friends, maybe not the right kind, but it was fun.

BEYOND THE FEARS AT REDSTONE

Huntsville, Alabama

The same old question that all construction men have to face every week and sometimes every day in "Why can't you find work closer to home, we need you here." Well, sometimes this was impossible. When being a steel erector, you had to be where the job and steel were. So traveling was a must. But due to pulling some invisible strings , I was employed at the Redstone Arsenal in Huntsville, Alabama. We developed this area into a strong hold for ammunition being shipped to our fighting men in both Germany and Japan.

We handled some very high explosive then. I still shake when I think of this dangerous and crude manner of supplying the great need. I was the trouble shooter for the entire plant, from the river to the front office. Hence, any breakdown or trouble happening, I was called to fix and repair.

I will never forget the suicide tube that was prepared for the pilots to strap to themselves while carrying the "Norton Bomb Sight," a very precious instrument to use and triple precious to our enemy. God forbid that our enemies ever received this machine that could direct a bomb from a plane into a barrel at thousands of feet above. This bomb-sight was sure vital to the early close of World War II. The machine itself was prepared with this tube of high and sensitive explosives tube to destroy itself in case of a crash or being shot down. This tube was of made of aluminum of approximately one-half inch in diameter and nine inches long. A small vibration or sudden jar would destroy everything in the whole area. The pilots would strap one to themselves so to be destroyed. This seems far-fetched, but the impossible treatment these man received forced many to tell of the US secret plant. So rather than talk and take a chance, death was chosen.

To make this high explosive and press it into small pellets similar to aspirin, we had a small metal building down in the far side of the plant area near the river. This building had strong concrete walls approximately four-feet thick and a loose roof just resting on top of the walls. So when the explosion came, it would only blow "up" and do very little damage. It was my job to keep it in operation.

In the center of the building there was a large pot that looked like and old-fashioned cooking pot, only this one was large enough to hold approximately fifty gallon of this important mixture of TNT and tettrel. These products were heated by steam at a designated heat, then stirred for so long. You may well know it could not be over-cooked or roughly handled. Our shoes had no tacks, our tools were of copper, brass, and lead, no belt buckles, and no watches. Nothing to create even a small particle of static electric currrent. Then this was pressed into these pellets and placed into the tubes for use.

I felt grateful every time I walked away from that building. At night, I could look at my family and thank God for the true care and protection for the day. It was very little anyone knew of this danger that rested so quietly in that place.

We loaded shells for large guns to destroy the enemy tanks there to the size of 155 mm that is approximately four inches in diameter, and 14"-16" long, these were loaded with the case and bags of powder and large shell in the business end ready to go, except the fuse that the gunner installed on the place of use. Sometimes this would blow up in the building where being assembled. I witnessed some very bad explosions there. It seemed was that the workmen there were so over-anxious to get the boys, the much needed material to help close the war as soon as humanly possible, that they by-passed all safety factors.

THE ATOMIC BOMB JOB

The challenges were sure great there and I left there feeling as I had contributed a small part preserving this great freedom we have here in the good old USA. While I was there, the contracts were made and I was in Oakridge, Tennessee at the great Manhattan Project or the Atomic Bomb job. This was the most secretly guarded job ever in the United States. We were checked out from before birth to get in there. Great expense and time were spent checking out not only our heritage, our patriotism, and our past, but our ability to keep a secret.

We dared not talk of even a tool or materials or any of the purpose of this major war plant. We were told if it worked, the war would be shortened. Our hiring consisted of approximately three days of briefing and warnings. I have many memories of this job in Oakridge, but I felt a cloud of gloom over me all the time there or even thinking of it.

During this war era, America was not free from sabotage. All employees had to be on a lookout for this all-important factor. Rather than traveling in and out of a job site so much, I chose to stay on the project day and night. On a very dreary day as we were walking from the dining hall back to work, the conversation led to certain individuals. We knew of men that we had not seen there that day. After questioning around, I heard they were sick. My stomach made to heave and I turned to my closest buddy and asked him to lock up my tool box, that I was leaving then for Gadsden, Alabama. I never walked back to the gate to leave that night. Just jumped the fence, walked to the highway and hitched a ride to Chattanooga, not feeling well enough to continue hitchhiking, I caught a bus for Gadsden. When I arrived home, I felt as if I would bust. I had swollen so I could hardly keep my pants closed. The first move was to clean me from that poison. Thanks to a good wife and doctor, I survived the night. The next day, I felt as I had been beaten all over with a baseball bat. But I felt well enough in a few days to continue meeting the challenges ahead.

On my return to Oakridge, I heard of men that died from eating the same chocolate pies as I had. Sabotage or not, God only knows. As I left the Great Atomic Plant, I looked back to see the large K25 Building connected to the Y12 Building knowing something new and adventurous was sure to happen. I had to say in a prayer "God, I pray that you will use it best." I didn't know that a select group was in New Mexico training to drop this monstrosity on our Japan enemies. The bombadier of this plane was a distant relative of mine named Thomas Ferebee. To read more on this, read the book "Enola Gay."

Today, this is a great research center for the good and benefit of mankind. May this continue to be funneled in this direction. There are many problems and unknowns to be solved in this field. May God raise up and use many of these young, brilliant minds to study and develop for the welfare of mankind.

WOMEN

When thinking back to the early 30's, and reflecting of changes that have happened in the construction trades of the USA, I feel blessed that I have witnessed the most dramatic changes that could happen. Many areas have taken a 180° turn. I will try and relate some of them to you.

In 1933, the construction man was an unusual person, a man that was unusually strong and durable, a person that did not fear death and hardships. There was a special force that made him stay in the game. If it was not his love for someone, maybe his wife and children, then it might be his car and home compelled him to go to another job site. Alimony or the sheriff made many steel workers stick close to a job.

Many times, workmen were fired and ordered to leave the job site after working only two or three hours. After driving hundreds of miles and the last of a money spent to reach a certain job, and the job last only a couple of hours, we wonder why.

The boarding houses were only a flop houses; there was drinking, poker games, and girls to drain the men's last dollars. This created some dirty fights and sometimes killings. The policemen in town knew all about every steel worker in town before he had received his first pay check. The cursing and language was like steam rising from a hot pavement. The morality was low. When crime happened, the first thought was, "Those dirty construction workers are in town. Beware!"

Now in the 80's, the change has been so great that there are even women and girls doing this work. The foreman, when he wants to assign a job on the work to be done, must try and be unusually nice and pleasant to the workmen. You even hear "would you please bring that package to this area sometimes when you feel to do so? If you don't feel like doing that now, you may go with someone else today." There should never be any harsh words or threat in his tone when requesting someone do a job.

I was on a job in Holland, Michigan, and the telephone company was called to change a phone line to another near-by building. A young girl and her companion came out to do the job. She weighed approximately 115 pounds and had strapped to her maybe 40 pounds of tools and harness. She followed the man for a half hour doing nothing. Then she was asked to go up that pole and cut the wire loose to be changed to another location. She climbed up the pole twenty feet and fell away from the pole and broke her back. I helped to pick her up and load her in an ambulance for a trip to the hospital. She did not have very many bystanders that were in sympathy with her. Later, she healed up enough to go back to the office and work. I will never know what was proven, in this case as in many similar instances.

LAST UNION MEETING

The last time that I attended a union meeting of structural steel local #340 in Battle Creek, Michigan, it was a sad experience. I could not see any good future for this one-time good local. The strong smell of booze made me wonder if this was the union hall or the devil's bar. Smoke filled the air causing the eye to burn like fire. The language was loud and vulgar. I had never heard such vile language, even back in the early 30's in Birmingham, Alabama. The cuss fights to and from the chairman to members on the floor was all wicked threats and filthy language. I had noticed a new member sitting there with some women drunk.

I was saddened by it all. I knew God could not and never would honor such a wicked gathering. Not long after this meeting, I read a letter that our local #340 had been taken over by the international union headquarters in Washington, DC. I was glad to hear of this act. Our local union leaders had removed from our treasury $170,000 within a few short years. The devoted union men that we elected to lead us could not lead themselves. This was another obstacle in the road for a potential steel erector.

How can men of this type represent a local union to receive and talk to executives for contracts? I could see the quality of men had decreased in both character and ability to perform, This makes it doubly hard to erect a steel job with the quality of men as we see now coming as journeymen and bridgemen. Yes, men have changed, unions have changed, and contractors have changed. The lust is gone for the old type steel erector.

THE WEAK AND PEACE

I shudder when I see and hear these young peacenicks with their picket signs and peace banners. I realize how very little they know of how peace is obtained, and the price many young men have paid so that they may have the liberty to protest against the establishment. This is sickening to me. I know most of my college football team was killed during World War II. The peacenicks are sitting back resting on their laurels forgetting the other generation of good men who died for the US. These men prayed and died hoping their children would never have to fight a war.

Getting back to WW II, Hitler was making good progress in Europe. He had France and England on their knees begging us to come and we could see we were next on Hitler's schedule. One faithful American soldier was asked, when he came home after the war, "What does that AEF stand for?" He replied it meant that "After England Failed" and that statement was true. The Japanesse saw that Hitler and his war machine were doing well, so they jumped on the bandwagon to riddle us from our west.

There were many sad, frightening days, months, and years that people in the know feared America's takeover. Every morning I expected to hear of Japanesse troops landing any and everywhere on the California coast. They had their inside machines working to discourage America from standing or fighting back. We were told every day on radio that it was too late for us. Don't let our young men die uselessly, etc. Same as the peacenick promote today. "Poor ignorant souls"

I have said this to try and state how much the USA was unprepared for any kind of war. The power plants were just enough so we could turn on lights in our houses. None for plants and factories to operate on. Power houses are not built overnight. It takes years even if materials are available. Guns were scarce. I declare if American people are not allowed to have guns and ammunition in their homes, "we are gone" both from inside and outside. Even Castro could come on up here and capture us with a walking stick in hand. I thank God for red-blooded men and women that know our history and are willing to protect our shores at any cost, and not to be a loving friend to our enemies.

There was a steel mill not far from Birmingham, Alabama, trying to fill orders for our Army and Navy without electric power, materials, and manpower. They were trying to operate and perform miracles with only a shoestring to do it with. There were only two companies that made turbines to produce power here in America. Republic Steel cried, begged, and prayed, what can they do to get a large blast furnace going. This process was very important to the manufacture of steel. We were called in to leave Gadsden, Alabama, to go to Canton, Ohio, where someone had removed an old-type turbine years ago. We heard that it was lying beside an old building there and we were to get it and bring it to Alabama and try to repair the damaged pieces and assemble it again for the use of a large blast furnace.

Off we started and found it under a large snowbank. The parts were not all there, which required trying to buy more parts, or if not possible, we had to make them ourselves. It's needless to say, America was desperate to survive. Well, we did all we could and thanks to a great Westinghouse Erection man that came out of retirement to help us with his dedication and brilliant mind. Very few people can realize the value of these dedicated men and women at that critical time.

We worked long hours, and got very little sleep. Sandwiches and coffee were our meals for weeks. One day we were ready to try it out. To put the steam to this machine was like trying to make an airplane and fly it across the river. We watched and listened to strange noises and moves. Remember turbine speed is over 5,000 RPM's. When the large 16 foot flywheel is making that speed at over 5,000°, it's dangerous for any one. This turbine junked in time passed but was now resurrected again for use. We ran it in for approximately twenty-one days, and had no trouble, Republic says, "let us have it, we need it now." When they accepted it, we left town. We were free from its future. My next job was in Panama City, Florida, so off I went, but in a few weeks, I heard that the turbine got away. The steam control valve refused to shut off the steam and the turbine kept going faster and faster until it was impossible to stay within the housing. It busted out and traveled hundreds of yards through the buildings going to a large scrapyard—just where it belonged. "A desperation move."

A RAPID PROMOTION

I was sent to Tuscaloosa, Alabama to complete a new plant for Goodrich Tire and Rubber Co. This plant lies west of the city approximately three miles and makes tires for tractors and automobiles, plus there's one division for manufacturing truck tires. There was one event that happened that I always relate to that job. I will try and explain the incident to you.

It seems that construction men always have a bad temper or get angry in short time. Well, along that line, I was a true construction worker. We were erecting a platform off the second floor. The platform rose approximately 42" off the floor below and a set of stairs led up to this elevation. All the floors were covered with 1¼" standard grating. I was working for an older person from Birmingham. In fact he was the president of local 92 of Birmingham.

Gillie was having trouble keeping his stair stringers on some elevation. He strolled off and left me there for a short while. During his absence, I measured the hole gauge that was important to stair location. When Gillie returned and hopped down across the beam from me, he stated that he knew where the trouble was. I nicely asked "Where is it, Gillie?" He said that those sets of hole gauges were different. This was exactly the holes I had measured while he was away. I reported to him "No, sir, they are the same. I just measured them." He bounced in there and said in a fit of anger that he knew damn well they were wrong. I told him clear and plain that I lived all my life to keep from being called a liar or thief and here he was calling me a liar about those four holes. I grabbed him by the head and neck and whipped him over the beam on my side and onto a grating floor. This I regretted badly, and began to try and apologize to him. I picked up his hat, dusted off his clothes trying to be nice to him. He picked up his tools and began walking to the office and left for Birmingham.

The sad part and good part of this kind of union job is that later, I met Gillie in Birmingham. He was the job steward and had the power to hire and fire. There was a large addition to the steel mill there and could have been a good job for me. But Gillie said "No," that I was too highstrung. I told him I did not think so, I just wanted people to treat me right, not calling me a liar when I did not lie. I thought for a few minutes that the Tuscaloosa event would be a rerun, but I left the job site without going to work there.

The football games there kept me busy keeping up with both the University of Alabama's team and a colored college there which had a full schedule of football also. At that time, it was an all-negro college and they definitely had a different way of doing things. I would attend all their games and laugh and laugh. All the team wanted to be the quarterback. They wanted to be the leader. All chiefs and no peons.

SNAP OUT AND SNAP IN

Gadsden, Alabama

There was a big load of steel for a building unloaded down by a funeral home that all steel men had their eyes and minds focused on. knowing that there were many nonunion men that would "snake it in" or put the steel up at a much lower wage, we would go to any extent to prevent this. So who got the job was important, especially to us.

Everyone knew that it was going to be a mean job or hard to get to between the buildings that already existed. The existing trees were in the way of a normal erection job. The road on one side prevented any entrance from that direction, and all knew it was going to be crucial who got the job.

Well, I was called to this job and went down there to give it a more serious look. We call these jobs "hand line jobs." They need good strong men and simple rigging. Well, I had chains and big ropes and wench trucks hanging on the side of all the trees in that block, some to keep the steel from drifting into the buildings and tanks, some to pick up the steel at the proper location for connecting to the other steel. We would not dare let these large steel beams ram into the old funeral home. The terrain was very soft and irregular and was hard to walk on and struggle around drifting the loads.

We had a good strong man, one of our best, trying to prevent any kind of accident, like keeping it out of the high power electric lines and existing windows, etc. Well, during this tough and crude move on one beam Gray pulled his shoulder out of its socket. He was lying down in a ditch approximately three feet deep. I climbed down to examine him and told him that I could pull it back in real quick but it would sure hurt badly for a few minutes. I told him to let us do that before it started swelling too much. We got all set to perform this act and he decided, "No!" Then off to a hospital two blocks away Gray was hauled. I called his wife and she met us at the hospital. There were two sisters at the Catholic hospital, and the doctor was on his way. So the doctor called the nurse to give him the *ether*, he would be there to reset the shoulder. This nurse eased around to me and whispered for me to grab and hold of Gray's left leg when Mary applied the ether to his nose. Mrs. Gray was to get the

other arm and the other sister to grab and hold the right leg. Gray was unaware of the plan. Mary, the sister nurse, had a sponge of ether and immediately placed it over his nose and mouth. This reminded me of catching and trying up a big hog in southern Louisiana two years previous. Big Gray flounced and flopped, throwing us everywhere, and jumped off the cot. He was out into the middle of the floor. He held up both arms and shouted, "Its in, its in!" during all this episode the shoulder slipped back to place. We got our hats and coats and went back to the funeral home to complete erecting this steel.

A WILD HOG HUNT IN LOUSIANA

The carefree style of living by these dear friends in Louisiana sure appealed to me. They never seemed to bother themselves with too much work. Long hours on the job or overtime were never a demand from them. I would always marvel at the answers I would receive when the employees were asked to work a certain Saturday or Sunday. "No, no. My weekend is planned. Let Walter or someone else who has a family that needs it do it." It was hard to find someone to work overtime eventhough the wages were doubled.

I very easily fell into that myself. The hot sunshine and high humidity in that area contributed much to this factor. But it was never too hot to fish or hunt. One year I was in the area and it was suggested that when the water went down on Bogue Chitto River that the wild hogs would come back to the swamps—and that Maurice Singletary and his cousin and myself should venture in that area to catch us a wild hog. Well, this sure sounded very exciting to my ears. I had always heard of wild hogs being in those swamps. These men knew them and their normal habits. A. D. knew the area far better than anyone in that area of Louisiana. Now A. D. saws and hauls timbers such as large cypress and southern pine logs from those places. He knows where they are, and when, and how to get those precious logs out. He also kept one eye cocked on the wild hog population and their whereabout he was also a good man to be with, so I listened eagerly to A. D.

The time arrived at the Pearl River that both the East and

West Pearl had gone down and Bogue Chitto was down and this week we could go in the big swamp.

I asked these men what would I need to make this hunting trip. I remember well the three items they told me. A good pocket knife was a must. Sometimes we may have to cut through jungle-like briars and vines. A pistol to have handy just in case we have to shoot him off. This sounded reasonable to me. No rifles needed. Too much trouble. And a tube of medicine that stops bleeding real soon. These wild hogs had tusks that would rip your legs open badly. Yes, I sure could see a possible need for that.

I could hear in conversations for days before our trip "If Ole Joe gets healed up enough, I don't want to go without Ole Joe. He usually will heal up in three weeks. He looks much better, I was by to see him last Sunday. I think he will be O.K." Ole Joe was the leading hog dog in Southern Louisiana. He was owned by a state senator that loved to hunt but seldom found time in his schedule. So these men knew Sixty Rayburn well and could borrow his dog. In fact, they trained Ole Joe to hunt. Joe was a Catahoula dog. Very little known of. This is a dog mixed with the dogs that De Soto brought to this country, and the dogs the Indians had when he came. They are found only in Louisiana and East Texas. There are regular Catahoula conventions held in or near Baton Rouge, Louisiana every year to show, swap, sell, or buy a Catahoula dog.

This is a special dog for hog hunting because (1) he can be vicious, loves to hunt, and (2) he has great intelligence. He will listen to commands, will turn loose of an animal if requested by a master. They know how to work with another good dog while they are attacking their victim. (3) A very mild and good tempered dog around children. Seems as they know how to protect and care for a child. For instance, when the kids are playing in the yard or near their house and guarded by a Catahoula, parents never worry about snakes or harmful animals harming them. Most of them have one white eye. They are not a pretty dog, but a great dog for that area.

These men began to talk of where we could get a dog to hunt with Ole Joe. Maurice had a cousin that lived near there that had a good hog dog. It was somewhat young, but had been out a couple of times. He also wanted us to take a younger dog to train to catch hogs.

Our time was set and we had our things ready to enter the swamp to catch us a wild hog to keep over to next season to eat. It was not a game merely to destroy. This was for special sweet bacon and sausage for next year.

Oh, I was about to tell you of a most important man made trouble for the sportsmen in this area of Louisiana. The Barnett Reservoir that covers many thousands of acres in Jackson, Mississippi area was built to protect the area of Jackson and surroundings from serious flooding in the spring. This reservoir contains the water until the authorities in Mississippi decide to release the water to go down Pearl River with a big bang. I have heard some of the men say they would be out in Pearl River in a boat fishing and lo, here comes a five foot wall of water from Boss Barnett Reservoir. No warning for this makes a person keeps his eyes and ears open to make a quick decision to cope with this all important element.

Now this was not an important factor to keep us on the highland. When we had Ole Joe, Tige, and Rip all in the back of our truck. We were towing a fourteen foot river boat and twenty-horse outboard motor straight to the Pearl River at a Lock I. We quickly launched the boat and up the river we could see the big fork in the river as we pulled into this area. I could see that we were approaching an island. We pulled in there and the dogs soon began barking as if they had bagged a big lion. Well, here comes four will goats running toward us for help. They seemed to be so helpless. We stopped the dogs and caugh the goats tied them up until we crossed a river on into some deep swampland. I stayed at the boat to tie it up as Maurice and A. D. hustled ahead with the dogs. Soon I heard the will chasse, such vicious barking from those three dogs made me know I should be up in that tall cypress near me. Here they all came toward me. The big hog was stopping and turning on those dogs, a very interesting sight to watch. The hog was slashing at the dogs and growling. The dogs were using every means to elude this attack.

On and on through the brush, briars, and water and mud the race was on. I sidetracked behind a large tree to let that show go on through. Things got quiet, A.D. says they have him bayed. This means he was contained by the dogs. We ran in that direction of the barking dogs. We found them in front of the large boar hog barking like mad. The hog was backed into a big patch of briars against a big log. He feared nothing from behind, and he could handle things from in front.

We planned for this occasion. The dogs kept the hog entertained by moving closer and closer one at a time. Where the hog attacked the closest dog, the other dog would pounce on the ear of the big hog. They were very careful and aware of those tusks the victim had, and could use so well.

Meantime A. D. moved in quietly behind the big hog with a short stick in hand, rope handy and all in one quick movement, had the stick in his mouth and the rope around his snout. He was giving the big hog a bear hug from his back. He was helpless when his tusks were "destinated" I had a good cross stick prepared to carry him out on. So the job was done, only if it would stay done.

We dropped by the island to get out goats and continued on out before dark would catch us in that wild area.

It seemed as we could hear a constant noise or something running from, or catching something, all the time we stayed in the swamp. The big snakes, the alligators, coons, muskrats, beavers and many animals I did not know, were fighting for their survival.

We crossed rivers and soon landed back at lock One with three goats, one hog, three hog dogs and three crazy men—all in one small boat. We gave the hog to a very reliable black man to keep and feed for us for the following year. This is labeled by this steel worker as good fun and great bacon.

THE ALLIGATOR HUNTS#1

You will hardly find anyone who will tell you that the swamplands of Louisiana are now tame and safe to travel through and swim in. Some of these Cajuns will try to tell you that all is well there and O.K. Don't believe it. There are still many wild acres of large water moccasins just waiting for some victim to come his or her way. If the victims don't come by, they begin their search for something moving in the water. I have seen may old rusty-back moccasins the size of large water glasses and four and a half to five feet long. Yes, these rascals are deadly poisonous, and their vicious ways almost label them as the ruler of the swamps.

The Bible tells us that since Adam and Eve the friendship between us and the snake was dissolved. There is still a living fear of snakes even today by men and women, "especially me." Maybe these Cajuns get more acquainted with them and get closer to them than a transplanted Yankee. When you talk of the Louisiana swamps, you must realize that nearby, there are snakes.

I was in Bogalusa, Louisiana during the late 40's trying to build an addition to a large paper mill. The summers there can get warm, even hot. The humidity there puts you into a perspiring state early in the morning. Sometimes you sweat all night. The first year I was there I noticed if clothers were left on a clothesline overnight, they were always wetter in the morning than when they were hung out. So some nights, even a hard working steel erector has trouble getting a good rest. The steel gets so hot sometimes you cannot sit on it. You can spit on it and it just balls up and runs off, as if spitting on a hot stove. So many days or weeks of this atmosphere affects a man's mind and he does not exactly think very clearly and straight. One day, a friend of mine came to me and very quietly asked me if I would like to go with him to hunt alligators that weekend. I have always had an unusual craze for excitement. Due to the many days of 100° F weather, I came up with an answer that should have required more thought than I gave it.

The following Friday evening, there were four of us lunatics riding deep into some swamplands just off the Pearl River. This river furnishes much back water through Louisiana and Mississippi with large alligators, snakes, waterfowls, and some of the largest spiders I have ever seen. Some get to be large as big coffee cups and have big red eyes that look you over, as you do them. The Spanish moss that hangs from those cypress trees sometimes touches the water. This provides a perfect habitat for the snakes, spiders, and mosquitoes by the thousands.

We drove a four-wheel drive jeep through old logging roads until we could go no further. George, the leader of us heathens, told us that a few days ago, he met his uncle in a bar in uptown Bogalusa. His uncle told George that the river, being as low as it was now, was a perfect time to go into ole Alligator Lake. He also told him of a pero in the Alligator Lake. A pero is a half log that has been hulled out so someone could ride inside it. Boy is that a dangerous set-up. When you are riding inside a pero and swap sides of your mouth with your chewing tobacco, you are in the water, because the pero has flipped.

When the jeep could go no further, the four of us unloaded. I had my new rifle, George had a rope. The other men had pistols and knives. George told to us that if we walked due east, eventually we would run into the lake. He remembered this from his boyhood days. We all had head lamps on our heads for light to see and travel by. We finally found the lake. We decided to split up; two men go that way and two men go this way. So George and I went this way until we found the pero or boat. It was laying upside down in the water approximately eighteen inches deep in the mud. So we started wading to the boat to drag it onto shore. Vines, moss, and mud covered it both inside and outside. As George was cleaning the boat in the pitch dark, I cast my head light across the lake to check it out. I counted the eyes of seven alligator in that area. The moss hung close to the water, and into the water many places. I was assured again that I was in the wrong place. This was a terrible position that I had gotten myself into. I prayed, "Lord, forgive me for making such a dumb decision as this, and please protect me through the night and this will never happen again to me." He did, and I did not.

When the boat was cleaned up, we climbed in, George seated in the front, and I sad flat quiet in the back. The water was extra calm, not even a ripple on the top, just like always before a storm. The only ripples were caused by a "kersplash" from the snakes falling out of the moss, or a beaver racing to safety. Excitement filled the whole swamp. The cranes were whooping, frogs jumping, and all beings racing for safety. Except George and myself.

George asked me which alligator we wanted first. We counted seven eyes. An alligator's eye is a large red eye that looks like a cow's eye. You can see only one eye because of his high bone ridge between. It was chosen by George that we go get the one on the far side. Since he had the paddle, in front of the big boy we quietly looked each other over. George asked me to let him use my rifle and for me to grab him when he shot him. I was ready to punt, but George sh—ot this monster and hollered to me to catch the rifle, which I did. This lake boiled and boiled just as if a large truck had been dumped into it. George cursed and I thanked God that he got away. If a bullet does not hit an alligator's head directly perpendicular to his skull, it only stuns him and he stirs the water. This one left that section of the lake for another area.

But these old troopers could not be defeated and it was on to the second victim. By this time, the whole swamp of hundreds of acres had come alive. There were chirps, groans, squeals, moo's and noises I had never heard before.

The number two alligator lay still waiting for our arrival. I could tell it was not nearly as large as number one was. We used the same procedure as before. George shot, I grabbed my rifle, and somehow, some way, my hunting partner grabbed the 'gator by his nose and rolled him in on his leg. He projected his right foot out into the water and used the leg as a logger would a skid. Over into the boat come six-foot alligator, flopping and fighting on top of me and my new rifle. I felt that he should have stayed in the water somewhat longer, but I was reminded that when he dies and the air leaves his body, he sinks to the bottom and we lose a good alligator.

We had fun around that lake for several hours, but I was so grateful to get our alive. I felt much safer atop of the tall smoke stacks or high buildings. I never bothered my good friend George again to go hunt aligators.

THE ALLIGATOR HUNT #2

Monday morning on the job, one of the men asked me where I was over the weekend. I told him that George and I went to hunt alligators. Parker told me that George would get you killed by those things, and that I should go down Pearl River the other way and hunt them deluxe style.

So off we went the following Saturday morning down the ole wild Pearl River to a sand bar in the bend of the river. Parker said "Here is a good place. There should be one in that hole in the bank there." He pointed to a twelve-inch hole. We had with us only pistols and a clothes line. I thought we should have had much more equipment, but Parker said no.

The sun was up now and it began to show signs of being another hot day. My good friend eased over to the big hole and barked like a fiest dog. We waited a few minutes and he repeated this procedure again. We drank a coke and again Maurice Parker barked into the big dark hole. I noticed that the sand began to shift around that area. Soon we saw the nose of a twelve foot alligator peeping out. Parker very gentlemanly placed the noose on his nose, and then his head, and when his front legs came in position, around them the clothes line went. We had a nice twelve-foot alligator all bagged and ready to go. In the forties, they were valued at five dollars for the first three feet and three dollars for every foot thereafter. So this catch would be valued at approximately forty-two dollars for his hide if properly prepared. At 1980 prices, he would be valued at approximately two hundred dollars. The meat now is very expensive and served at most restaurants in the New Orleans area.

FISHING IN FEAR

Fishing with Tom

Where I had been used to fishing was from a small boat casting along, or maybe we'd park the boat under a big tree that provided a good shade over the water. There I expected a few fish to come in to the shaded water and cool off as I would do. Well, I didn't catch many fish that way, but I didn't hurt myself fishing either.

I must tell you of my favorite fish story that happened in the area of Varnado, Louisiana. Tom Smith was a good welder in the shop, welding and fabricating almost anything needed. I knew him as a good welder, but everyone else in four adjoined parishes knew him as a super fisherman.

One Friday morning as I passed his work station, he called me over to tell me that now the river was down low enough for him and me to get in there to an old lake. We had talked many times of going there when the water lowered enough to locate it. So then we planned our strategy. The time, place and equipment were no big item to settle. The next morning was a beautiful Saturday, and fishing was the number one item on the agenda. Tom and I got a real early start down the river. We traveled over dead tree that had fallen across the stream. The birds and animals gave us a signal that we were disturbing them far too early. This river "push-pa-pap" was known for its large population of moccasins. They are not my favorite pet. We traveled over and around and through some rough situations for approximately five miles. Tom signaled that we stop here, that he thought the lake lay over to our left. He told me to stay there for about twenty minutes, then climb out of the river and travel east and enter the lake casting from this or the west side. We would meet somewhere near the center where the water was shallow, not over our heads. Sure, we waded in the river and in the lake.

    I cast several times in the river where Tom left me. I had already caught seven nice big bass. I was beginning to believe that those snakes were as afraid of me as I was of them. I tried to find comfort in that. When I felt my twenty minutes were up, I began wading to the bank of the river to climb up on the bank to view a total new country to me. I reached for a limb on a large cypress tree, and there lay all coiled up was a large moccasin, and his tongue was spitting toward my eye, but he never struck or bit at me. I usually keep a pistol in the tackle box for his kind, but I figured that since he left me alone I would leave him alone. I climbed out and the tall reeds were over my head, but through it all I could see Tom coming my way. There were small muskrat trails running throughout the dead grass, I had to move out of the trails as I walked to let six big snakes coming my way like mad pass by. Tom was running those vipers over to me. I promised God everything just to let me get out of there alive. I even told Him. "Don't ever let me get into this situation again, even better you should put me in jail or anything." I saw Tom step off into this lake on the far point. I did the same on my end. So we were to meet casting along. Yes, we caught more fish than I had ever caught. All Louisiana is filled in with dirt and silt. There's no rock in Louisiana.

    This lake was bottomed with a soft white clay, so while walking through, my feet would settle down sometimes to my knees, in mud. The water came up to my shoulders and sometimes to my chin. There in that area lies a small mud snake-like viper. I have seen them; they're approximately three-feet long and they live in mud. They are also deadly poisonous. I could feel them as I would remove my foot for another step in the mud. This happened several times that I would lift my foot up to release one of these lamp-eels. I prayed that he would go the other way. This was the most dangerous and exciting day I had ever lived until then. We had the most beautiful string of fish I had ever seen, but never again did I even suggest to Tom that we go back in there and catch some more.

RIGID RULES

Bedford, Indiana

Just a few days before Christmas in 1951, the Farabee family and the Lee family were located in the Limestone Capital of the world. Bedford, Indiana had been good for us. First, it gave us a chance to compare the schools of the north against the schools of the south. This had always been a very interesting subject to me. The teachers and school faculty were great to us in this unique and lovely city.

The job had been a very unpleasant one, due to the overzealous steel workers sent to our job from Louisville, Kentucky. All the men quoted me the union rules, as if it was all Greek to me. I felt as I knew the rules both front and back so I could see some that these men were going to straighten me out on this Bedford job.

My previous fifteen years at this type of work had me well prepared to cope with most any kind of manpower. The job superintendent had decided to pour concrete in an area on the far corner of the plant layout. This happened to be the toilet area when the plant was completed. But now the superintendent wanted a concrete slab on the floor to build a temporary tool shed and place for us to change clothes. When the concrete truck arrived, the steel erections all stopped to go put the wire in the toilet area. Six men and crane all stopped for approximately a fifteen minute job for one man. You may well know my blood pressure rose but, I chose to hold my tongue for the present time.

The building was designed for many columns approximately thirty-five feet high. The connectors had been riding the hook to position themselves atop each column, a very easy procedure and which the foreman may or may not permit. If the foreman says "no riding the hook," the men have to go to climbing the red iron. Some men have a terrible struggle with this. The union rules read, "not to ride the hook or load line unless its absdolutely necessary."

When the wire mesh was installed and the concrete poured in the toilet area, I reminded the men not to ride the hook any more, just climb the steel, and was there a bunch of riled steel workers from good ole Louisville. So all quit or returned to the union hall. I started the next day with a new gang and after a few words of introduction, the job started again and proved to be a good job for us all.

I mention this to remind of how narrow we sometimes let our minds get hiding behind a big bear called the union. The Bible in the Spiritual world cause these people a novice.

STREATOR, ILL.

When the job was complete in Bedford, we were thinking about Christmas. My boss from St. Louis had me scheduled to report to Oven, Illinois Glass Co. at Streater, Illinois as my next assignment. There was a large building to be added to their warehouse area. I first had to locate the city on the map. Yes, its located in the heart of the corn belt of Illinois. The soil is rich and black throughout that area.

The normal procedure of the transition from job to job was that I go first and get the layout of the job and arrange for an apartment or house to move the family. I traveled throughout the whole area for a week and found nothing. I begged, I prayed, I promised, but the final decision for me was to buy a trailer. These were years when only the trash or cheap undesired people lived in trailers. When you told someone that you lived in a trailer, you dropped your head and said it real low. So Friday night I drove back to Bedford to prepare the sad news and uncertain trip to move my good wife and four children to a new home.

Trailer

When I reported in to Louise that it was impossible to rent or even buy anything in the Streater area and I had purchased a trailer, my wife stood for a long time with mouth open and not a word came out. When the voice came back all I could hear was, "No, no, no. Can't be." I tried to console her but to no avail. By the next morning, she asked how big was it and where was it, how close to a school, etc. I told her it was twenty-eight feet long, and eight feet wide. To use psychology, I stepped off the twenty-eight feet in super-long strides, but I was not convincing enough. She kept howling, "It's impossible, it's impossible."

When we settled down to face the reality, the first and tough question was, "What can I do with my hope chest?" This was a good question because it had been with us for so long and I know how attached to it she was. We had moved it many, many miles over several states. This bothered me, but I remarked that we must sell it for what we can and try and forget it.

Remember, my wife and I were alone until our children began to enter this world. Louise's mother died when a young woman and her grandmother let the three children come and live in their home. So there was never a real established home for the children.

The Farabee family had nothing to offer in a time of this second crisis. The Depression days had us scuffling to the first necessity, food. In fact, during these times, Louise and I made contributions to my mom and dad. So a place to store my wife and four children for a few months was impossible.

I have told this story many times of how the impossible can be a blessing. Monday morning found us traveling to Streater in the big bronze Hudson automobile. The temperature was 20°F and falling fast. A bad winter storm was coming out of the northwest. The cold rain turned to an icy sleet. It froze on everything it touched. I was pulling behind me a luggage trailer approximately six-feet long, with a canvas cover over it well tied down at the corners. All our belongings were under that canvas tarp. This was a terrible drive in the slosh of the black dirt freezing where it touched. My windshield was covered, I only managed a small peephole for driving. I prayed constantly that this trip would be a profitable one.

When we reached the Streater city limits, all of us exclaimed "Awe, no!" I drove through town over a small hill and on the next hill was the sales lot where I had purchased the new home for us. The trailer was frozen in about eighteen inches of ice and snow and could not be moved until the spring. The subzero weather kept coming;—20°F (below zero!) by the next day, we were not geared for this weather. We still had on our Louisiana clothes. They were sure too thin for this storm. We began living in the trailer that day of 20 below zero. There was no running water and no sewer for the waste.

The woman that hollered so loud only three days ago proved to be more than a faithful, true-blue wife and mother. We sat inside the trailer and cried for two days, trying to squirm around. This seemed great to our kids. Not many had the privilege to live in a trailer we would say.

My wife was just super great in how she coped with this impossible problem. She was not a well woman physically, and not a natural acrobat on ice. A few days later her bad teeth had filled her complete system with poison, until the pain was unbearable. But even though she was suffering from the terrible pain, she would always carry in all the water we used from a nearby service station and take out all the waste. She kept the clothes all washed and clean and maintained the normal clean habits that she had had instilled in her since birth never weakened or dimmed. The children were so great during that time, no TV to stare at, no friends to escape to. So we were all locked in for the winter. When spring came and the job well completed, we were transferred to the New Orleans area. I believe the best steel men I ever used were at Streater, Illinois. A good group of men. The building was to be riveted and good riveters were there. These men came from a Chicago local which I was very grateful for.

When I see trailers now and all the room there is in them, I thank God again for the experience in this area. I do believe this experience brought our family closer together than anything else that has happened.

HURRICANE IN LOUSIANA

During my travels I have seen much damage done from the hurricanes that came regularly out of the gulf. They can be depended on to come out two times a year, generally during the seasons when days and nights are the same length. I happened to be raising steel for big buildings and installing machinery in the southern part of Louisiana one time when the weather man warned us about hurricane. This was a big one and due to center over us at ten o'clock the next day. There were men from all over the South as far away as Nashville and Chattanogga and Little

Rock working on the job. I told them all early to scatter or go home, don't be there when it happened. They did as I suggested. I was living there with my wife and children and had to ride it out. The morning of its arrival I was checking out and tying down things on the job site preparing for the big blow.

During this time, it was discovered that the large smoke stack that reached approximately two-hundred feet into the air had been damaged on its side and was leaning across the turbine room and power house that supplied electrical power to the whole area. The officials came to me screaming, "Can we do anything to keep it from falling?" We had two hours before the big blow was to arrive and it was not coming in the direction to favor us.

I called out three local men and made up a large strut or system to connect it to another nearby smoke stack. Anyway, at 10:00 we were on top of those smoke stacks two-hundred feet up swirling around in the air trying to save the plant and much equipment. When the storm passed us it was clear as could be, but dark as pitch minutes before it hit.

We came down to the ground in perfectly fair and calm weather. No harm had been done to property or man.

This provided many interesting things to tell about in the bars, and as groups gathered, we admitted to each other about what fools we are to do these things. There must have been a great God looking down and feeling for such courageous but dumb men. I can understand now, that He guided us through many, many storms.

As I review my experiences while erecting steel buildings, bridges, and doing mean rigging jobs throughout these United States, I realize that the contractors felt that men's lives were cheap. The value of property and time was premium. This condition requires that a man was to work harder and take more chances. When they begin to take chances with your or another persons life, let it be known that you can't win them all. Some will die, some will remain crippled for life. Families of the victims suffer much and long. Thank God for more safety laws and unions that do stand firm to protect the employees health and safety.

UNKNOWN PREPARATION

My Dad made a living, or almost a living, digging coal out of the mountains in North Alabama. For fifty years, he struggled for us so we would survive in this world. I don't remember all he told five of us boys, but I do remember that he asked and also told us never enter those coal mines to work. This was repeated time and time again. Well, none of his sons did go into the mine for a living.

But, the wild, courageous, red blood we had in our veins would never let us sit by contented and watch the world pass.

My background was roaming hills and streams, climbing cliffs and trees, and never turning down a challenge to or from anything. I dreamed of the days I would be old enough to play football, and this did happen. I played high school and college football, never losing a minute due to injuries or not being physically ready. This was quite a feat, considering sixty minutes playing both defence and offence in padding that was the very minimun. The hobo days mixed in with football helped prepare me for a steelworker's life.

While playing football in high school, I played with, a very close friend and fine young man by the name of Howard Bachus. He was a natural athlete approximately six feet four inches tall and weighed approximately 215 lbs. while in high school. You could look at him and know there was an Indian not far back in this heritage. Some days I would go home with him for dinner. So many times his mother would be busy and tell us to just help ourselves. Howard would go through the house and come out on the back side with two large pieces of corn bread in his hands, a salt shaker in his pocket. We'd go straight to the garden for food. He would gather radishes, cabbage, carrots, tomatoes, and back to a wash bench to eat. This would all be washed down with fresh cow's milk .

I thought it was pitiful to have to live like that in the 30's. Now every medical book says to do this for a healthy life. The best for fiber, vitamin A, or disease fighters needed in all our bodies. Plus the meal was not cooked to death.

It is sad to see how most children eat today. Pop, candy, and potatochips are the leading killers among our kids. Parents wonder what makes their kids so hyperactive, and feed them this junk.

"We are exactly what we eat." Some women and girls prefer not to eat "very much" and their resistance to diseases is not "very much."

My physical condition has never been found lacking due to our manner of living. The hobo diet was largely fresh from gardens. The exercise was a must and very complete. This kept me working continually on steel for forty years, never losing a day due to sickness. I got hurt, yes. I was bruised up several times and could not go work for a few days. But I am healthy.

So many times we refuse to eat, but that is necessary to enjoy being a healthy and happy person.

NEW ORLEANS

I was sent by local #58 in New Orleans to work on the John Manville Celotex Plant. This large plant was on the west side of the muddy Mississippi River. Not being used to this area and its fast procedures, I learned another very important lesson. We worked hard and long to put a large tank in the ground and get it covered up. This job lasted until nearly dark. When we arrived back the following day, the tank was out and on top of the ground. We did not have it filled with anything and the buoyancy from the ground was so great, the large tank was forced to the surface.

These Celotex panels were made from sugar cane squeezings or plummings. This is the remains left from the stalk after the juice was removed. This was the basic for the insulation. There were many tons of that stuff there, an area as large as a football field and thirty feet high. Well, we did some reckless welding, and this stuff set afire. I ran up to the local firemen shouting fire and they would not leave their card game until it was over, and by then the fire was nearly over. I had never seen anyone so unconcerned that was being paid a wage. I began to wonder if all those Cajuns were that irresposible. Thank heavens, no. I found some of my best and realiable men were Louisiana Cajuns.

The Huey P. Long Bridge that spans the wide Mississippi River is a most beautiful bridge. This is not a suspended bridge as many good bridges are. The Goldcen Gate Bridge at San Francisco and the great Macinaw Bridge of Upper Michigan are suspended by large woven cables, that continue across high and mighty towers and end up toggled or anchored into mountains or some other solid anchors.

This Huey P. Long Bridge has large piers coming up from bedrock that supports this long type bridge. The army engineers, when it was designed and being build, said it was foolish that it would never last, never withstand the radical changes of temperatures that create much expansion. There is a railroad running down the center of this bridges and regular truck and car traffic on each side. When you cross this great bridge, you will marvel at its structures. This was built back in my early days, and engineered by super craftsmen. We must consider and pay tribute to the past generations of great mechanics.

A bridge high enough to clear the most of the largest ships that sail the Misissippi. A bridge strong enough to span the widest place of this great river off pins that give it a large design. A bridge strong enough to withstand the strong winds from the north that follow the river basin from Canada. A bridge durable enough to let the icebergs that flow down the river in the spring, striking and removing anything that gets in their way. A bridge that carries the large trains, both freight and passenger, down the center of it with hundreds of tons going east and west. I am thrilled at this great feat for the engineers and the steel erectors.

The Charity Hospital of New Orleans

We were in this area doing a job when the Board of Directors of the Charity Hospital in New Orleans became fearful of how the building was leaning over. I think it was nine inches that it was out of plumb. We were asked for a bid on bringing it to its right position and preventing this to happen again. This was a very heavy stone building approximately ten floors high. We viewed a set of the drawings of plans for the footings of this building. I was amazed how far it was down to rock or something solid enough to work from. Louisiana is a filled-in state. Its a long way down to solid rock. We refused to get involved with this job. We were not prepared with equipment or knowledge of the water tables, properties of the clay, and other factors.

TO LIVE AGAIN

I had rather someone else tell this story but its up to me to put it in print, so here it is as it happened in a small paper mill town in southern Louisiana.

I was working for a construction company from St. Louis, Missouri as steel superintendent. We had many different jobs of various types going over the entire plant. I had approximately fifty steel men on the job; some building, some wrecking, and a big rigging gang moving large machines and vessels around. So we were busy throughout the plant.

A company employee came running up to me and gasping for breath told me that one of my men was unconscious in the bottom of a large tank. I knew of the vessels he was referring to, but could not visualize my man being there. But I ran over and up there and there was a man down approximately forty feet below in a tank. I prepared myself with a rope around my waist, another dangling loose inside, plus I pulled my shirt off and tied it over my nose and mouth to breath through. I could smell a gas collecting there.

The story ends where we pulled the man out, that the gas inside the vessel had overcome a friend, Lester Maghee. We gave him artificial respiration for approximately twenty minutes before I felt a strong pulse in his arm. After a few moans and groans and a trip to a nearby hospital he came around great. A good father to three children saw many more years due to a courageous and defying act. After much serious thinking and talking with his dear wife, he helped establish a gospel quartet, a gospel singing group to travel over the country singing and telling a testimony of how God had opened his eye and changed his paths into a beautiful life.

HARD TO SWALLOW

Some of the greatest people I have ever known lived along the Gulf Coast. Men that were true, never told you a lie or misrepresented any facts. They worked hard and loved their families. We would gather on the bank of rivers, lakes, or parks and have picnics or "crab boils" and shrimp suppers. The catfish fry was a time loved by all. Men and their families could relax and enjoy themselves out of doors. Not very many gatherings were enjoyed as this. The beer and whisky were not a part of the lives of these men and their families. These were the most rewarding years of my steel-erecting career. When I visit that area now, the nights are not long enough to reminisce about the old days.

I received a special invitation one hot August day for my wife and I to attend a chitterling supper. This was a special event attended by many of the city's elite preachers from the nearby area. All were scheduled to gather and eat chitterlings. I knew well what chitterlings were, but I was not noted as the greatest eater of those things. As the time drew closer and closer to the big day, my wife kept saying "I'm not going, no I'm not going one step down there." Well, I kept saying that I am going, and we did.

When we arrived, the smell provided the proper location of the activity. After meeting many people there, I though I would visit the back of the house and see the proper system of cleaning the chitterlings. I noticed one thing that I did appreciate. They sure used lots of water. This dinner was not chitterlings only, It was backed up with southern fried chicken and fried frog legs. Mrs. Louise Farabee ate chicken legs on this particular day and chicken legs only. I began as some others, standing in line away back by the tall pine trees. But I have never been treated as nice as this. It was most gentlemenly group. Everyone would say, "You go first. I know you were ahead of me." Yes, I was just as nice as they were. When I got just inside the door of this large kitchen, and the warm air and heat from the many cooking pots plus the smell convinced me then I should have listened to my good wife and stayed home. A big burly man from Mississippi was handing the chitterlings from the pot. He recognized my head coming in and shouted out, "Ole Red Farabee! Here are two good ones for you!" I thanked him but please be sure not to let anyone go hungry for chitterlings. He said he had enough for seconds and for me to hurry back. Well, I began to gather in all the trimmings as hush puppies, onions, pickles and all the dressings I could find. I cut off a pieces of one of these chitterlings and began to chew. I kept the trimmings close to the bite as I could, I had planned to swallow it soon and suffer from it the next day. Well, I noticed that I had waited too long for that game plan because it was now too big to swallow. I fed that hunk of chitterling to a nearby hog dog. The next bite was much smaller and swallowed sooner. Just in case you don't know what chitterlings are, they are the outside liner of pig entrals. Same to a pig as tripe is to beef.

We sure had a good time with those people. I learned a lot about them. That I was just about as good a chitterling eater as the majority of them. It's hard to find a good chitterling eater now in this area. But if anyone could eat them, it would be a dumb steel worker.

ACID RAIN

Acid Rain

Seldom can a newspaper be read without an article about acid rain. The news reporters can always rely on this being a very interesting subject to everyone, not only in the United States and Canada, but over the entire world.

The quiet and lonely fisherman in the uppermost part of Canada comes home saddened by what he saw in the most beautiful lakes. Some are resting up in mountains where no rivers or streams run into them, but dead fish are found there caused from the acid rain. Some lakes are so clear and clean that fish can be seen 60 to 65 feet under water swimming around near the bottom. Sometimes the nearest city is approximately 300 miles away. But signs of the acid rains are present.

We hear now of the same problems in Europe, especially in the northern area. England and Ireland are reaping some problems caused by this long-range killer. We even hear echoes from Japan and Australia. Seems as the complete world is now affected by this acid rain.

The extent of this problem is not known yet. I will try and relate a few harmful effects it leaves behind, and its causes. Paints on cars, and buildings must be unusually durable to withstand this enemy. Especially aluminum products are marred and actually eroded away in a few hours when in contact from the acid rain. Now many buildings are designed for the outside skin to be of aluminum due to its light weight and strength plus an unusual beauty, but they are soon marred and eaten away.

The cause of acid rain is traceable back to most all of our cities that have power houses, or where electric power is produced. The grade of coal is being used that fits the cities budget, and not the good clean air that we love to talk about. The coal used by the hundreds of tons in each and every power house has an ingredient within called sulfur. When the coal is burned in the furnace, there is a by-product left, some in fumes and some in ashes, called "fly ash."

There have been many provisions made to try and collect these bad properties of cheap coal, but none have proved to be a complete answer. All kinds of filters are designed and installed, but somehow enough fumes or sometimes ashes escape and many innocent victims far away are troubled by its effects.

The power companies build tall smoke stacks to force the deadly smoke higher and higher. This only causes the trouble to be transferred to points further away.

One answer is the nuclear reactor to produce the steam for the turbine that generates electric power. This system is unpopular with a large number of people. I do feel as we must accept the new system, but take every precaution to control it and place the nuclear reactor in far away places in case the worst happens. There are many improvements to be made in this field today.

But as a steel erector, I place my thoughts back to the erection of the high smoke stacks that you see while traveling across our country.

As we gather together in our clothes-changing shanties on these construction jobs, the men talk freely. There are many other jobs discussed. The dangers, the usefulness, the cost of jobs from various opinions of engineers and workmen. I have learned all these opinions are worthy of exploring. When the big smoke stack now in Douglas, Arizona was being discussed, I wondered why so large and so unusually high. Sixteen hundred feet is equivalent to a 150 story building. What kind of a base would it take for this structure? What would the effect of the hot weather that is sure to be present in the day time be? How would it respond to the cold nights? So many factors had to be considered and complied with before the job began. The general purpose of its size was to get the fumes up and out of that area. The proccesing plants were willing to pay the expenses to clear the nearby area. But recently, I learned while being in Douglas that the farmers nearby are paid not to farm. This is due to the harmful effects of dangerous smoke and fumes.

DEATH STRIKES AGAIN

Smoke stacks, I have found out, can be dangerous and costly. Many men lose their lives trying to earn a pay check on these things, to take home to their wife and children.

I remember well while we were erecting a stack in Holland, Michigan. This stack was to be a 450 feeet high. 36 feet at the base and 13 feet outside at the top. This was made of concrete and steel. The company out of New York received the contract to build it.

They were definitely a large and reliable company to build this type of stack. A big job had just been completed near Austin, Texas by this company and the same gang came to Holland or the men who were left. The turnover of these stack gangs is great. Very few men start on these jobs top them out. This is due to several things. Some say the money is too small, a stack too big. The mental attitude of *another* stack job with new men is frozen to a flat "no."

The refusal of a man's family to let him work on another stack keeps many at home with their loved ones.

As we started this job in Holland with a job superintendent from Texas, I rated him at the first conversation. A man of much zeal, but little brain, a very dangerous type of man to have on a job. To have this kind of man in complete control was a shaky set-up to start with.

Old man Sid brought in with him only two men, one man from Houston and another young man from Memphis, Tennessee. It did not take us long to shake hands and get going on this four-hundred and fifty-foot smoke stack. We were to pour 7½ feet of concrete every day we worked, after we got set up. During the first week, we had several changes in our personnel. I was a leader for the top crew, or to lead out with procedures. I definitely was responsible to "old man Tex."

Tex had lots of promises, but never offered many true answers to problems. As we were going on up with the stack, it reached 100 feet and the safety of our lives began to diminish.

Every day we pleaded for a new type and more scaffolding inside this stack, but due to one day delay from our regular 7½ feet pour, the time would never permit the safety of our working conditions on top. We kept going on up praying that nothing would happen to us.

Herschel and his family came from the Memphis area. The young man brought his wife and small daughter here to Holland for this job. The closeness on the job led to a close family friendship. They visited in our home several times and our friendship grew close. One night they visited us and left with a water heater and things I gave him to complete the necessities of life for a few weeks here. The living quarters here were very crude, supplying just the basic needs to survive and not suffer. They had a small child of approximately five years old, ready for a year of school in the northern part of Alabama. We marveled at the fine up and coming family. Herschel had an eye that was not just right. It had a cocked eye look. He could see through it O.K. but it was very niticeable to others. His wife and he had discussed getting it fixed, and a doctor in Memphis was scheduled around Christmas time to do this. One thousand dollars was needed to do this and Herschel just told me that if we kept working regular that by Christmas they could have that much saved for the operation. If good weather prevailed, it could be done.

The next morning at 10:15 Herschel slipped from below me into eternity. We had had a good brotherly conversation for approximately one hour, about the smaller things of life.

Seeing this happen does have it effect on others. I usually withdraw for a time, and get a general look at the complete picture and try and collect good from it, and try my uttermost that this never happens again. These kind of happenings make us all consider other means of attaining a paycheck, but within a few days, I am back again.

There are many, many of these happenings that I have witnessed of my close friends. It is sad, but somewhat expected. When we all entered this kind of life, this was the first point mentioned. A short life is sure. This is why I am writing these pages now, that I am so grateful to God that I have survived forty years of this rugged and dangerous life. It has left me with no pains or serious injuries to endure my remaining days. I do have many sad memories and many good and rewarding lessons. So steel erection has been good for me.

I have always tried to maintain clean and healthy living habits, trying always to invite spiritual things to all I come in contact with. I've encouraged others to read, study, and live the teachings of the Bible. That this was our only hope for a full and abundant life. Just same as in the time of Jesus Christ, some listened and some didn't.

Well, we completed the stack and later there was another one built near it reaching 650 feet into a clear blue sky. To me, these are beautiful. I can see in it the hard and dangerous hours endured to erect this monument. This is a payoff or a very rewarding sight.

Even though these stacks reach to this height there are still acid rains. The sulphur in the coal plus the rain water makes a H_2SO_4, as this strong acid destroys most all that it touches. While I was with General Electric and their slogan was "Progress is Our Most Important Product," I asked them several times, "Is this progress?" Sometimes our so-called progress besets us. So this makes our future bright for inventions, changes and improvements. So the fields are white for our young intelligent minds to bring about and develop a new and better system to produce electric power.

This is not only true to cure acid rains, but in all phases of life, medical, transportation, structures of all types, and foods, Even our social lives could be improved on. I am trying to say the big gates are open to you for great potentials.

RUN, RUN, RUN OR DIE

Poison Gas

We were sent to North Muskegon, Michigan to erect a building for a chemical company. This building was an additon to an old structure that was almost eroded from the strong solutions and fumes. This gas produced by their loose system of handling a very deadly gas gave me the shudders. When we entered the plant gates on a beautiful Michigan morning, we were all asked to gather at a certain area to be indoctrinated in the plant rules.

We construction men are somewhat a different people, especially the steel erectors. They can be led anywhere, but not pushed or compelled to do anything. We must know or be convinced that what we do is best. Our lives have been jeopardized so many times, and we have seen so many sad things happen. Sure we get doubful of others opinions. This makes us very dogmatic and firm. When our lives are at stake, it's foolish to be other wise.

To be a good erector requires a person to be an engineer, a chemist, a metalist, and emergency doctor, a counsellor, and a machinist. He must also be in good physical condition. It's not easy work. The man with the blueprints in his hands advised us that they made a product there that was not good to breathe, that we could not *see* it, we could not *smell* it, but we must be aware of it. Our orders were to run when we heard the *three whistle toots*. I asked where do we run to? The answer was that there would be someone there to point out the way to run. The direction of the wind determined the way, and we must get away from the invisible gas. The first symptoms of its presence would be that our eyes would burn and then it would almost be too late, that you could already have some in your lungs.

I looked to the east toward a woodland area. I saw large trees of all kinds, but no leaves on any of them. Not a very selective direction, to the east. It seemed as this might test our track skills, as to our length on this job. I looked back toward the men that worked for this chemical company. I noticed they did not have anyone but young men there. I asked "where were the old men?" A very honest question, but very confusing to try and answer.

I looked toward the job site of this new building, and many large containers and lines were labeled "FOSGENE." This was a chemical that had a deadly ring from my past school days. Yes, my first act when I arrived home was go to my library and look this word up. Sure enough, all the information stated, "a very deadly gas used in World War I, against the American troops by the German." This gas affects the eye and is deadly when it reaches the lungs. There is no known treatment for it.

I had two choices knowing this, either stay or go. I prayed all night about the decision that I should make. I knew If I stayed, my respect for myself would be great. I felt as my knowledge and determination to respect this fosgene gas might lead to saving lives of the other workmen also. I called the chemistry professor at Hope College to brief me as much as possible on this gas.

The professor told me not to bother or fret about this. This product was not around in Michigan. It could not be possible that it was that near a city or that the sloppy method as I described was used to produce this product. I answered that it was, and he could join me the next morning and I would show him. He didn't come, but I returned to the job to erect our building.

We were organized to drop and run at the first sign of a leak under us or over in old buildings. A quick warning of TOOT, TOOT, TOOT saved our gang from much harm. Several days we would have to skin down columns for three floors and run as many as four and five times. A very exciting job it was.

I hope you can understand now how that great mass of people in India died from this product. The inability to warn people of the danger that lies in their faces. The deadly effects, the lack of knowledge, and no preparation to treat patients all leads to, "Why did it happen?" Now many eyes have been opened to this problem.

Our labor unions do fight and fight hard to prevent these things to happen, but I say again, if *we are aware* of harmful effects it is one of our safety escapes.

THE CLEAN AND EFFICIENT POWER SUPPLY

My knowledge and experience with power houses and methods of producing electric power are the turbine that are run by water power. This is an old long-time system used. We see many on rivers and streams such as the Tennessee Valley Autho-rity, (TVA). These are simple and not expensive as other methods to build. These dams and power houses that lie on the big and beautiful Tennessee River are profitable to many. The farmer profits from the control of the river floods. The cities profit from the cheaper rates for electric power. The sportsman loves the great fishing and hunting in and around these beautiful man made lakes. The construction of these dams happened during Depression days to help provide jobs for the needy and hungry. This was a great move as many types of labor were needed. Surveryors and helpers, and anyone who could swing an ax and was not afraid of snakes and the wild could go to work. Next, many cemeteries were to be moved, knowledge was provided of where the low lying areas would be, when the dams on the river were built. So many things were changed as homes moved. Some small towns or villages had to move to higher ground. So any able bodied person could go to work that needed work.

On any other type of power houses, only the skilled trades or mechanics are needed to do the majority of the construction. So unskilled men are limited to modern construction to a great degree.

This waterfall powerhouse must have a good and suitable topography required. So they can be limited also. A very rare type of powerhouse was built on lake Michigan just south of Ludington, Michigan. I think this is a very neat and profitable system to follow. Again, the setting must be appropriate. The topography must be suitable. The soil and clay must be the proper type and depth.

A general purpose of this job was to pump the water from Lake Michigan into a large homemade lake up on a mountain or larger hill. This lake was to be approximately seven miles long and one hundred feet deep. It had to be large enough to hold trillions of gallons of water. This water stored in the upper lake provided a sure source of power at the proper time to the needed. Most electric power is used after four o'clock in the evening until 10:30 at night.

We all know electricity is hard to store except in batteries. This water is released through large gates and flows to turn large turbines that in turn produce electric power. This sounds simple but much engineering, planning, and expense are required to do this. But when this type of power unit is installed, the expenses to operate are unusually cheap.

When I left the Ludington job, I was told only sixteen men could handle the complete process, and that was for all shifts. No coal was needed, no reactors for dangerous radiation was used.

STORE ELECTRICITY IN HOMEMADE LAKE

I was very fortunate to be one of the first construction men on this job. We started digging near the shores of Lake Michigan. The soil was to be hauled away to another area. The big hole was to be approximately 95 feet below the water level and over 600 feet long running along the shore line. This was a very treacherous task for the soil will be 90% sand and being dug at the base of a large sand dune.

The hole was almost completed when the rains began. This is what we prayed would not happen for a month or more. It's needless to say that our hole began to fill up with sand from the hill on the east and water and sand from Lake Michigan. We were down 90 feet below the lake level trying to pour concrete for the turbine pump foundations. A large crane used for handling materials was in the lower level with us. The continual rains were mixed with lightning that never seemed to let up. The three-hundred foot boom reached up into the center of those clouds. That created another danger of lightning following it down to us. Decision making time was coming soon. A good friend of mine, Walter, was in the hole with me at this decision making time. We had an order to try and get the 1/2 million dollar machine out of there onto solid ground. This was impossible as the only way out was travel out by the lake only to create more troubles sooner. So we decided to climb out up a large pipe to safety and leave the complete job and machinery up to God to care for. So we left the job site.

The next day we commended God for a good job. The big lake had not completely filled the large pit prepared for the turbine bases.

It is hard to comprehend the large area and dangers that were at stake. It was the same as two football fields end to end and sinking them into the ground one hundred feet. And on one side was a large lake, and a three hundred foot mountain of sand on the other. It seemed as the wrath of God hovered over this job site for approximately three weeks. It was a gloomy and troubled start on the Ludington pumping storage plant.

After the first winter things on the job began to look up. The bad weather and the wild winter storms had moved on away from our pet project. The men had begun to change from restless workmen to good reliable men. The attitude of the employees is very important in the amount of work received, plus the quality. Men that are not happy are unhappy. The weather is sure a vital factor in meeting a time schedule on a construction job.

Again, these Michigan winters when working near the lake will kill you. If you fail to get sick from pneumonia or freeze to death, there will be someone by to talk of Florida, and you leave the job. We were struggling to make a mean or tough connection one day in Muskegon, Michigan. We were giving all we had to complete this phase of the job. One of the men relaxed and asked us to just hold on, that he had to go get another coat. He was gone far too long and we were all about to drop. I asked the man's buddy where in the world was his coat? His traveling buddy said that he had left it in New Orleans!

This Ludington job was most unusual to work on, not only the topography, or the engineering of it, but the fact that all materials and machinery were shipped in from Japan. This was a shock to many red-blooded American boys that had seen their most treasured friends and relatives die from the Japanese bombs, shells, poison, and knives. Some had spent many months in captivity in the far east. You may be assured this was always hanging over us. I had worked many jobs we called the war project such as the atomic bomb plant, or "The Manhattan Project" in Oak Ridge, Tennessee; the large powder and TNT plant in Charleston, Indiana; large gun plant in Canton, Ohio, and many other places. These all were centerd on one general plan and that was break the back of the Jap, and to think that only a few months later we were taking orders from them on our own soil. This was a tough hard pill to swallow.

But we managed to complete the job approximately two years later without very many incidents that involved a clash. I do remember that I sat on top at the upper lake as the first water was to be pumped from Lake Michigan. This was a very exciting time for all. The bank was filled with Japanese engineers and their super good cameras to take pictures of the first water to be pumped by their country's products. I had prepared a good location just over the #6 flume, the one to be used for a try out. These men nervously darted in and out crowding me in my long-time position. One young engineer related that this was the most exciting time of his life, *and just think, it was all made in Japan.* I told him that this was not really my most exciting job, and I also related that the atomic bomb job was sure thrilling to me. The conversation stopped and I took pictures as I pleased.

PIONEERS ON STEEL

The steel worker received no training. The steel man is immediately set to work to perform the work he is paid for. The dangers are commonplace and just part of the daily routine. It is up to the individual to handle the problems from day one. In the past, a strong young man who was both dumb and smart, and had a desire to listen and work made a good man on steel. He must be strong enough to toss steel beams aside as if they were toothpicks, dumb enough to try the impossible, smart enough to make it fit together and work perfectly and have no problem, courageous enough to climb icicles high into the air and hang a large tarpaulin from one icicle to another in a 60 mph gale at subzero temperatures and come down smiling. He must be strong enough to drive rivets with one hand on the riveting gun and the other holding to steel while 30 feet in the air. Sometimes he must hold one man out to maintain his balance so the particular operation can be done, working above streets so far down that cars and buses look like toys.

He must be tough enough that the cold (-20°) or heat (110°) has little or no effect on his work, always ready to do the work designated at any physical price. I am reminded of welding steel beams together with poor shields and wrong shades to protect the eyes; burning or cutting steel and no goggles on the job to protect the eyes; no shields or goggles to be found while grinding off chicken droppings high into the air; hanging on a loose beam and no sign or type of safety belts; sometimes riveting inside a tank or smoke stack and no sign of ear plugs as protection for the ears.

These are a few of the working conditions that pioneered the conditions of today. The difference is great. The machinery today is dependable and powerful enough to handle the loads. If in doubt, no man would use it. He would just go home and draw his unemployment money and forget work. Well when there was no unemployment money for you and you had a good wife and kids at home waiting for you in a cold room to bring some bread and beans, the beans would be there.

Just a few more thoughts that ran constantly through the old Bridgeman head. When someone asks about the wet days how and why do you work like that on that high steel? I always sum it up like this: "If you were hungry enough and there was a piece of bread up there, you would go and get it."

SWEET REVENGE

After many long days of sitting in the bathtub rubbing out my right leg thinking of what the future might hold for me, I'd think "Revenge, Revenge to the Atlanta Steel erectors." I felt bitter, but unable to do much about. Then I realized I must work some place and soon. So out of the battub half healed, I drove to Atlanta and reported in to the company again, still on crutches.

They were gracious enough to put me on a job at the Federal Reserve Bank changing elevator doors. I was to change them from opening on the right side to the left side. This required much drilling and tapping threads. This was great for me and I could earn my wages there. I gradually began to return to somewhat normal health.

Several weeks and I was at a point I felt I could make it on some other job. I had to admire some of their leading foreman, they were good men well-qualified for any type work. "Good bridgemen," I became acquainted enough with them so that I said when I left Atlanta and located a good job for them, that I would call them. Well, the day that I realized that I could climb a column again, I asked the office for all my money plus the personal tools I had lost and broken on their job. There was much profanity used there about how much they were depending on me and I would treat them like that. That I was a no good so and so. I kept cool and smiled inside about this departure and felt much better leaving this way than the time before.

My next employment was near New Orleans. I inherited a good job there and I say inherited because that was what happened. The group from St. Louis, Missouri, all got in their car and drove off, went home, and left me holding a big job that had a tight time schedule.

This was not unusual that the construction personnel would all leave on the spur of a moment, maybe because of the uncomfortable feeling on the job due to conditions back home, lack of confidence in the men on job, weather contitions or many other reason could cause a group to "go home". So the job was left for me to complete.

Somehow my thoughts would cling to the good men in Atlanta. I called them and told them of what I had found there and to come to the job now for all the work time they desired at double time "driving riveted." They all drove in by Monday morning ready for work. It was a good job for them; they loved the job and made much money. They completed the job and left happy. I was glad for them and myself, but the chief in Atlanta sent me word "If I ever came to Atlanta again," I would be a dead so and so. Sweet Revenge. I almost closed him up by stealing all his good leaders.

Sometimes it's hard to understand the conditions that bothered and helped the pioneer steelworkers. The experience in Anniston, Alabama was amusing to me and tells a balanced story. I was sent to Anniston to work for a construction contractor. The office was from nearby Atlanta. I was sent from Local 92 in Birmingham, Alabama. Anniston was in union Local 92 territory for work. So the contractor was to abide by Local 92 working agreement.

The warehouses of a large government complex had burned down and we were replacing the steel. This contractor had poor equipment to work with and not much money. Legally he brought some men in from Atlanta; he knew them as a previous employees from other jobs. This was fine, he was allowed 50% of this kind of help.

The crane broke down and we were idle for a length of time, in fact, all day. This is hard for any foreman or company to live with. We were paid wages as long as we were asked to stay on the job. The second morning we came out and were told to go home and come back tomorow the crane would maybe be fixed by that time. The Birmingham men left for town, but his men from Atlanta stayed on. This was not a happy situation and we could not reason with the chief. The next morning the crane was ready. It was a beautiful day and all was ready for *setting steel,* but Pug and I from Birmingham decided that this was not the day for us to set steel and caught a free bus to explore the big government project that covered miles and miles of buildings.

Approximately three hours later we came back on the job site and met a very unhappy boss. He was fuming, cussing, and spitting all that a man could do and not blow apart. No steel had been set. Pug got behind me thinking it was coming to blows and he being an ex-convict and on his good behavior was not eligible to fight then and there. So I kept telling the great white father that this kind of behavior was not good for his blood pressure, but I don't think he heard. He paid us off in cold cash up to the minute. We walked approximately 75 feet and went to work with *another contractor* installing overhead doors. We had a good long job there and the chief had to order some more men .

The importance of good harmony on any job cannot be over encouraged. I believe the freedom and excitement found on construction jobs helped keeps me active in this field.

THE LA SUPER DOME

When the name of New Orleans is spoken every one knows that while in that city anything can happen to anyone anytime. If you have been in New Orleans, especially in the French quarter, you will notice that the girls stay painted and powdered up like clowns around the clock. This is for a purpose. These girls spend much time and effort to entice or draw men close enough so their wallet can be drained. They are pros at this and very few steelmen can pass this way and not be taken. Usually an organized group lures the victim to drink, dope, robbery, and death.

Many men I have known never report to work on Monday morning and no one knows why and no one cares. They are missing in action, maybe in the great muddy Mississippi, just a few feet away.

But New Orleans is a city of excitement, organized to get the money. The gambling games look so sweet and innocent. Friday night after paychecks are dealt out most all construction men cash them in at these places. Many of their wives know this and meet their husband there at the door to try and get grocery money from them for the next week. It's sad that a person can be so strong and powerful on the job, yet be so weak and easily swindled, off the job.

I have worked in New Orleans several times and worked with good hard working men that knew their jobs. The last job I was on in New Orleans was the great Super Dome. I left Holland, Michigan as the cold bitter winter began to arrive. It seemed as that the cold got colder by coming across Lake Michigan. I knew it got faster. The month of November gave a small indication of things to come. After several winters of hanging on these skeleton buildings up and down these lakeshores, it's hard to think and talk straight.

I heard a man say that it's getting cold and he was going to get a set of snow tires. When asked where he was bying them, he said New Orleans, and off he went for the winter. This is what I did the year of the Super Dome. American Bridge Company had the major contract. The literature we read from the company stated that this was the most dangerous and treacherous job they had ever taken.

This job being downtown created a bad traffic problem while under construction. It was hard to get to the job on schedule. Remember that in New Orleans all the water that falls in this area must be pumped out. This is for two reasons: a) it's below sea level or lower than the Mississipi River, and b) the tough grey clay soil will not let any water penetrate it; it just lies there as in a clay pot. When a person steps off into that mud he never pulls his boot out with his foot in it. The boot remains in the mud to be retrieved later. This condition helped make this an umpleasant job. So the manpower turnover was great. Men from all over the USA came there for a short while. This was a good well-handled job, as best as could be. Due to heavy rains, sticky mud, traffic jams. and fender wrinkling parties, all who worked there will remember it for years. I thought the most memorable sight there was eight huge cranes resting down in the center of the area on blocking or huge tracks. Their booms reached 325 feet straight up into the air to support the inside ends of the huge trusses for the dome roof.

These cranes were equally spaced and held individual sections of the building until the center section was installed. When the center was properly installed rigidly made up, all cranes could be removed. I thought this was great. Eight cranes much higher than a football field is long, straight up holding approximately 80,000 lbs. of steel each.

The 99 bath tubs that surround the top elevation to retain the water is an unusual construction. The large area it drains, and the heavy local rains makes this a problem to give much thought to. The water must be handled or pumped into the river and not just let it run off. Each individual section or "tub" weighs 44,000 lbs. and there are 99 of them. Many unusual factors were a must to design this stadium for this area. This is worth a visit while you are in New Orleans. Don't miss seeing this engineering feat. I felt privileged to be a part of this Super Dome.

WRONG DOES PAY

While I was trying to heal up from the Atlanta crash, "or fall," my right hip and right leg needed more complete exercise than I was giving them. So I planned a trip back to Atlanta. A fellow steel worker from Provo, Utah named Ernest, and a good neighbor, he was going with me. We planned to drive to Atlanta. Each of us had, or thought we had, a little something to do there. So we left for Atlanta, 120 miles one way, for nothing. We had a good day there. Earnest had his bourbon whiskey together in a big bag. He had his tongue going faster than the Oldsmobile that I was driving. It was about dusk and I ran a stop sign. I struck another car that had four people in it. I say *had* because I knocked them all out of the car over into a small park. There were two men and two women, but not one was married to anyone in the group, but all were married to someone somewhere else. Normally this is a bad situation, but this was great for me. Their car was demolished, none of us were injured. My head lights were turned around but that was the limit of damage to my car. Earnest hid his whiskey in a drain pipe in a nearby lady's yard. He kept talking and I called the police to the scene. I had to go to court. The bond was $149.50 to free myself from jail. We all pooled our money and this relieved from jail until court time a few weeks later. This car splash did not contribute anything good to our dwindling and almost dried up bank account at the Farabee residence. This fact plus the crying wife of seven months pregnant pointing to three young children that needed so many things that were not there, encouraged me to hit the road early, or before I should have. So back I went to Atlanta the next Monday. I demanded that I go back to work with the same company and on crutches.

Earnest was sent to Georgia Tech College welding and running hand rails at various areas on the campus. So we stayed at the

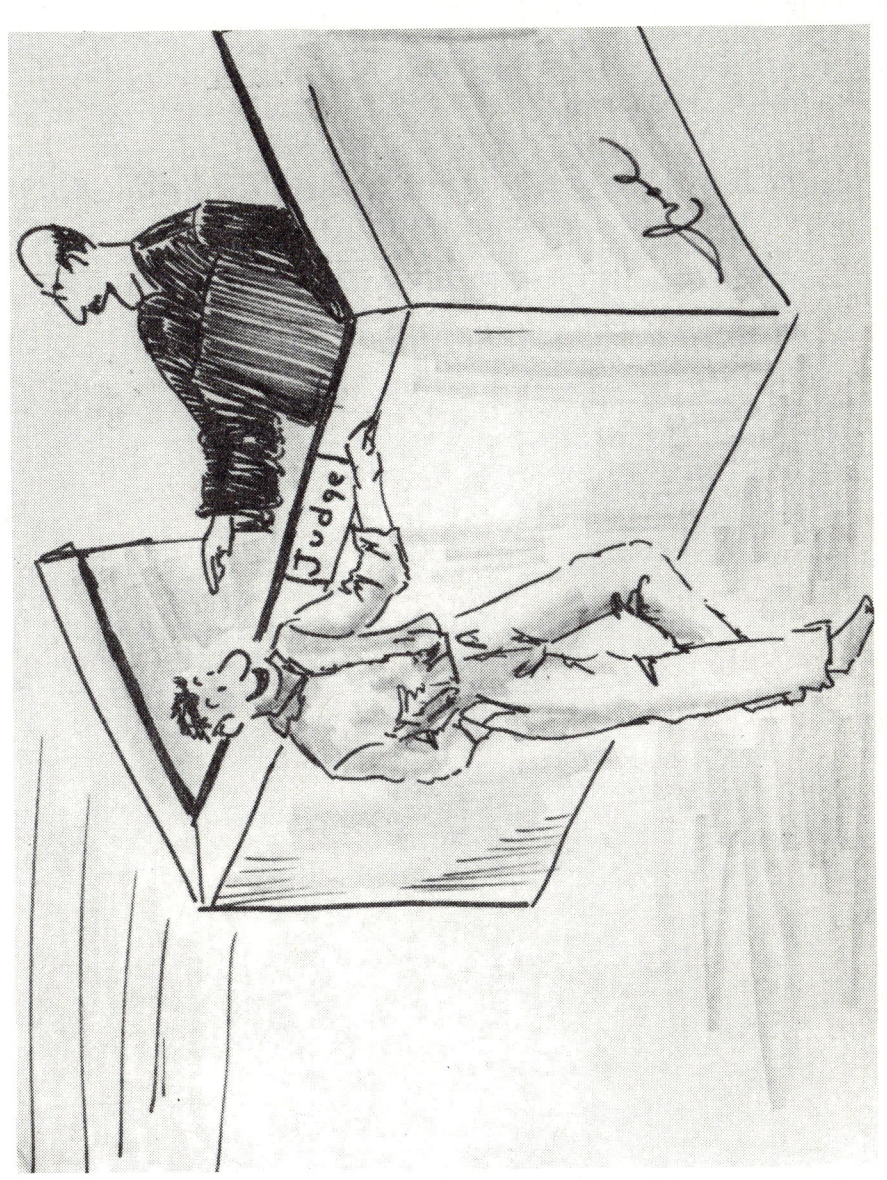

Tremont Hotel together for rooms and meals.

I was allowed to go back to work at the Federal Reserve Bank with the same contractor that I was employed by when my accident occurred. So Earnest and I spent time together discussing our future in court.

When I was free from jail and my bail was completed, home was our next move. We had used up approximately four good hours there in the Atlanta jail house.

As we left the front entrance heading to the sidewalk at 12:30 a.m., a strange thing happened. Earnest said I can't hold my water any longer and stepped into a large hedge and began to "wash it down." Out jumped a large policeman and grabbed at us. Off we ran down the sidewalk. I asked myself why I was running? I had done no crime. So I stopped running, but the cop ran Earnest to a stop. Back to jail for four more hours for Earnest. We got a bondsman to get Earnest out of jail and finally went home to Alabama. We had our time in court the same afternoon some three weeks later. We talked freely of its potential outcome and I was terribly concerned about my friend's day in court. He was worried about the decision from the judge about my car troubles. So we got up a small bet that I would come out cheaper than him. Trial time came and I was in traffic court. A long line of violators stood very quiet and worried, most were black men being held for some traffic violation.

When my time came to face the judge he looked at my papers and said "I see you are from Alabama had a wreck in Georgia." I said "Yes sir, your honor." The judge asked if it was my fault and yes it was, but I had straightened up all damages and settled with the others involved.

I had paid the other parties $100 for a $1,000 job just to not mention names. I said "praise the Lord" this is one time "wrong did pay."

The judge looked at me and remarked that Alabama had the best football coach in the nation and had just fired him for nothing. He had won six championships for Alabama. I remarked that the man responsible for the good Alabama football team was the man now coaching the Miami, Florida professional team, a great line coach, and unsung hero. Boy that judge jumped up and said to me $10 for having a wreck in Georgia and we kept talking football as I left through the door. I always felt as the judge must have been a brother-in-law to the coach. I left the court room clear and clean, but $10 lighter.

Earnest had papers from some quack doctor in Utah stating that due to a previous fall while on construction of steel mills in Provo, he could not hold his water and was apt to go anytime. The judge sure laughed about this letter and Earnest coughed up $35 to make him happy. We laughed much about this event.

ANOTHER SAD DAY

I was in Grand Rapids, Michigan on a job for a contractor from Chicago. This was a good job and had good employees. It was only a twenty-five minute drive from my home to the job. We felt as if we could use another good man. We needed a welder and called in the Local 340. A few minutes later a man came out that I knew real well. I knew his brother and oldest son. I was glad to see him driving in to our job. Joe Taylor was a good all-around bridgeman.

We had a coffee break at 9:45 a.m. but Joe had no lunch, no money, no coffee. I divided my sandwiches and coffee with him and we enjoyed our lunch together under a large tree. Joe told me that all he owned was inside that truck there, and pointed to it. His wife had run him off and threw in all he had, and that was only some dirty old work clothes and steel workers belt and wrenches. This was really not an unusual situation for our craft. It happens regularly.

We had not been back to work over thirty minutes when Joe fell five floors into some steel beams and concrete blocks below. I was on the fourth floor and he fell by me. I grabbed at him but failed to catch him. When I reached the body of Joe Taylor there was only a quiver in his body. The body lay smashed within a few feet of where we ate together and had a heart to heart discussion about personal life.

I called Joe's brother and related what had happened and asked him to come and follow through. Somehow Joe's wife was notified and out she came to get the truck and insurance money. I refused her the keys and told her of Joe's last words.

The next morning real early I received a phone call from Chicago and I was asked not to let anyone go to the job site as they had, due to an earlier error, neglected to have insurance on the Grand Rapids job, but all would be O.K. in a matter of hours.

It was all straightened out. But this was one more reason why structured iron workers need mean and powerful business agents. Who else can, and will protect the victims?

I have said many times if their wives only knew and cared of what the steel worker endures and the unreasonable chances that are taken with their lives that things would be better for all at home. But men will not go home telling their wives and children of the near death experiences that have happened even that day. Some of the calmest and best hearted men I have known have been pushed into a corner to death or total ruin due to a selfish inconsiderate wife. This has been a factor present for many years. No communication between man and wife and this brings out selfish "me" attitude that remains throughout the remaining life. The continual trouble. Some men quietly submit to this overriding power and some fight like a king cobra at every chance. There are no winners.

THE IMPOSSIBLE FOOT WARMER

After following steel construction throughout the United States, I felt as if I had met the worst conditions for a man to endure. Once we were in Port Sheldon, Michigan on the eastern side of the cold and bleak Lake Michigan. I knew it can't be much colder there than in Siberia. That cold wind coming across the lake never stops. The storms from the northwest continually keep coming. We were trying to erect a large coal burner power house there that reached approximately 225 feet into the air. The skeleton of the building was up, but not bolted together. The connectors had left it still loose. The temperature was 0° degrees this morning and dropping fast. Some of the men that were real real hungry tried to last out a few hours of time for expense money. When you drive a long distance to work and cannot work, it is very discouraging. So every effort was exerted to make some time up in the steel. Snow and ice covered all beams and places of work. The 50 and 60 mile an hour winds howled through the framework of the building sounding like fire wagons.

By 10:30 this morning all men left on the job had given it

up for the day except Kolean, myself, and a gang of four Indians. The Indians were from Montreal, Canada. They were good tough bridgemen. Communication between us was almost impossible, only the regular steel workers symbols and language could be understood. But these men were hanging in there. The snow everywhere on the job site was from four to five feet deep, but we felt we were dressed to stay warm even at -10°. Kolean and I were beginning to get cold at noontime, but decided to stay as long as the Indians stayed. They were working over approximately 150 feet away and up approximatley four or five floors. Soon after lunch I noticed that one of the Indians had slid down a column to the ground. I say to my partmenr that they are going home "let us go too." We began to let our tools down on a line and peel down the column ourselves. When I went down I looked back toward the Indians and saw the young man sitting in the snow, shoes and socks off his feet, just rubbing his feet with snow like a wild man. He said it made his feet warm. I felt as if I knew of a far better way to make feet warm. I say "come on Kolean follow me," and home we went. The young Indian climbed up the icy column to continue his work.

MUCH MATURING NEEDED TOBACCO OR RED?

One Sunday I checked by at the Greystone Hotel in Bedford, Indiana to see if the man that I had ordered from the Louisville Local had arrived. I walked into the lobby and noticed two men come in, one a large man approximately 6"2' leading a dog and carrying a shotgun in his arms. I knew that this could have been one of the men I had ordered from Kentucky. I approached the big guy and he was proud to see me. We really hit it off well while we were together. I found him honest, humble, helpful any way possible.

He came from the tobacco country. His father's life had been raising tobacco and helping his family chew it. He had his own recipe to cure, sweeten and make it in large blocks for chewing. The next weekend this big man brought me some of the especially fine chewing tobacco. It smelled so good I thought it would be tasty for breakfast.

The snow had begun to fall there in the limestone country.

This began to encourage us to rush on having the job up before Christmas or the weather would force us to close for a time. I was walking throughout the building area with a new chew of the special tobacco delivered to me. I was feeling great. I was wondering why I had not had anything like that before in all my life. That tobacco we had in Alabama was nothing like that. I kept looking up and talking to various men on the steel. By the time I had reached the crane area at the lower end of the building, I realized that much of that juice had not only run down the outside of my neck, but on the inside too. I saw the complete building start swirling around and again around. I had to get down on my knees and hands to hold the building still.

I lay there like a big hog until I emptied my breakfast, that was followed by my supper the night before and soon I made it up enough to reach the shanty and pull myself together. It seemed as only snow water could be kept down into my stomach. My tobacco chewing sure slowed down and in a hurry. I had good tobacco for sale.

This big man would go quail and rabbit hunting every day. The dog, gun and tobacco would leave the hotel for the nearby fields regularly. This sounds rare or even silly, but the other men rested in the bar drinking and fighting until they closed up.

ANOTHER GOOD LESSON IN DETROIT

Detroit has always been a good area to locate work in when most all areas are idle. Due to the automobile industries the steel mills in and nearby have drawn many plants and industries to Detroit. So if there is no steel going up in Detroit, there is just no steel going up anywhere. Local 25 in Detroit had always held strong for a good scale on wage pay, so when work was scarce, I would think Detroit.

I know this sounds like a very disorganize vocation with no assurance at all, yes it is, but I learned real soon in my life that I did not have things in my life under control. I knew the One that did have control over me. So I have leaned heavily on the Great Provider the Holy Bible tells us so much about. It is so simple, even a dumb steel erector could grasp it. As is stated, Christ knows his sheep and they know him and I have definitely felt this in my guidance, even from job to job. It's comfort needed by all, regardless of vocation.

Once was a famine, no work in the western section of Michigan. No large buildings were going up, no power houses being built, but the Farabee family still expected to continue to eat and preferred to stay warm while eating. This pushed me toward the Detroit area for a job.

I was so fortunate that our daughter Ivol, and her family lived in that area. Sure I felt that I had neglected them for a good visit. The two children and their mom and dad needed to know and understand their grandpa more. So off I went to Detroit seeking a combination of job and visit.

It was definitely good to be in their home again. Richard Kloote was working for the Century Insurance Co. during daylight hours, and attending the Detroit School of Law at night. This is not an easy task but Richard was a man of good health and much stamina, and having a very supportive wife, thank God he complete law school.

But, one morning while in their home a very strange thing happened that has caused all of us to look at our lives more realistically. Dick awoke early to begin his day at work and the strange feeling within his chest proved to be a hole in a lung. We are so grateful that we have someone to take care of us and all proved out that the hole was healed, and we have all been careful of the smoke and impure air that enters our lungs since. As we all know, if there were no valleys, there would be no hills. so we must learn and profit from the valleys in order to enjoy and sing praises from the hill tops.

STRONG CONNECTIONS

The ties or relationships made with these men can never be handled lightly or forgotten. Let me try and explain. During the rough and fierce winter months of the Port Sheldon steel job I met a special man in an unusual manner. There were men there from all over the US. Some from Florida (can you imagine their IQ). Some were from Canada. There was a group from Texas came up to make a few good pay checks.

We were busy on the steel trying to get as much done as

humanly possible. The terrible weather conditions made it unbelievably hard to accomplish much. I bet that something bad was going to happen. I knew it would be impossible to pass through a day as that day and nothing bad would happen.

Well it did, I saw a man from Texas fall. I knew where he fell there were many large reinforcing rods sticking out ot the concrete footing on one foot centers and the size of 1 1/4 inches. These rods projected up from the concrete approximately six or seven feet. The snow had all this covered, but this is where I last saw Tex fall. I ran over and found this man only as God had placed him there. His arms and legs and body were woven through the mass of rods and no serious injury what-so-ever. The heavy clothing protected the body from even a serious cut or bruise. I said to Tex "Only God can fit a man in a place as you found yourself." Tex left the Port Sheldon area to work in Flint, Saginaw, and Detroit. The move was lucky for him and he settled into a good job there. Finally he was the business agent in that region, and a good one. He become a hard nose who ran that section of Local 25 with an iron hand. They were tough on boomers and few could ever stop in that area. I mean to say not many out-of-town steel men ever worked in Flint or Lansing, Saginaw during Tex's rule.

But the exception to the rule always came and when Red Farabee came to that area, there was always a job for Red. Tex even provided Dave, our youngest son, employment during the summer months while he was going to college.

The stories behind so many buildings, bridges, or structures never make the headlines of local papers, but I marvel at the real men, strong bodies and big hearts that made them possible. Sometimes the greatest has only one line in the papers about him and his death, but the stories still roll around the shanties on many construction jobs.

THE LOCAL 58 LABOR DAY FLOAT

We had a good size job going strong in the small town of Bogalusa, LA. The steel was going up at three different locations. Two rigging jobs had several men employed. All the personnel was happy and working hard. We had two riveting gangs driving rivets like mad. The job was definitely a strong union job and all was going well.

I felt that on the coming Labor Day we should enter a nice float in the Labor Day Parade. I talked it up between several of the men on the job, and all were pleased with the thought. When all the suggestions came in of the type of float we should enter, we all became more excited.

The Local 58 structural iron workers and riggers float would be one of real bridgemen going through town driving real hot rivets into a steel frame welded on top of a lowboy trailer. This required an air compressor to supply the air pressure to the riveting gun. So the compressor on which we'd be towed along needed a full pledged operator to maintain. The forge to heat the rivet was anchored up on the high part of the goose neck of the trailer. The plans began to fit together in our minds—now to get them all to fit Labor Day was another problem.

Our plans were to use the regular truck driver Eddie Lee to drive. We had the truck tuned up to run smoothly and not stop along the route. When the float was being made, we left two small slits for Eddie to see out of and follow the two men in front. These men were dressed in full apparel for steel erector. The belt, wrenches, hard hats, and all the gear normally carried by a journeyman.

All steelmen cannot heat rivets and throw them accurately. So the ones that can *are rivet heaters.* The rivets must be heated to a desired temperature, not too hot. If too hot, they will not enter the hole, and if so the life of the metal is gone. If too cold, they are too hard to drive. So the heater naturally tosses out of his forge the ones that are burnt. Red hot and sparkling they are cast away to wherever to cool off.

The day of the parade came, and I reviewed in my mind things that had or had not been done. First, I thought I don't have insurance on anything out in town or on the street. So we must be careful, I prayed help us Lord! This can be a good day for us local 58 men if all goes well, and if not I could visualize fires caused by the hot rivets, kids run over on the parade route, many bad thoughts.

I had selected the most reliable men we had to execute this adventure. As you have gathered by now that all you can depend on of iron workers is *that you can't.* This sure makes things in

The Parade Float

teresting. So here is what really happened.

The float looked great, well-designed to relate the true action. "The bridgement at work," it said. The heater came out still celebrating the holiday "all drunked up." The complete group was feeling great from absorbing too much ruckus juice. The men walking so straight in my vision were reeling and stumbling along. The truck driver's eyes were in Eclipse and he was trying to drive the complete assembly with a fuzzy mind and foggy eyes.

The vote had been made on all floats and ours was second prize. I was glad to hear this report and prayed these good things would continue for us. But something failed us. The heater at the forge decided his rivets in the forge were too hot, and began to throw them out on the hot asphalt road, making holes in the street. The kids tried picking "those pretty red things" up. A scary start in a beautiful parade. The men walking in front carrying the American flag and our Local flag began to reel and rock under that hot Louisiana sun.

The truck driver could not see them and to shorten the story all of us finished somewhere far away from the rest of the parade. Eddie Lee had the long truck and trailer and all our goodies blocked in an impossible situation over in the Negro quarter where I had never been. It required much serious planning to get us out of there on to a road again. Eddie took our float home with him to rest.

Ben, our oldest son aged ten , was riding on the float watching it all. I truly believe that day Ben decided for sure that his vocation would be anything but this. I heard of several children that had burned fingers, but we had no serious accidents "thanks be to God"

THE WRONG LINE

We were doing a construction job for the prison in Jackson, Michigan that will stay in my mind for many years. As you will know, the prison life and steel workers' life relate very closely. Some feel that the steel workers that are now on the street should be in prison. But at this time our gang was free to go home every day at 4:30 p.m., but had to be checked out at a special gate prepared for us to go and come through.

We had a man working for us that knew more about the Jackson prison that the leading guards did. When we needed some special information or equipment Larry always knew the where's and what's. He was well-acquainted with the guard and many prisoners there. The rains kept coming and the job site became muddier and muddier. So we were all thinking or where our boots were. Most of the men had their own boots, but not Larry. He felt fortunate to have his own pants.

Larry was always eager to leave every construction job. He would be the mumber one man to all checking out clock alleys. Most every day he was ready before the clock hand had reached the 4:30 mark. So there was always a time of waiting before the guard would open the gate to let the construction men out to go home. This exit lane was side by side of a prison group going someplace.

The 300 lb. guard came up in front and looked down the long lanes of men and shouted that "all the convicts line up on the left side and all the construction men line up on the right side." No one moved. A few minutes later the big guard came out looking down the line of construction men and yelled out again all convicts get over in the left lane and construction men line up on the right side, looking straight at Larry standing #1 in the line. Larry looked at the big guard and shouted back "Hell don't look at me, I ain't no damn convict." The big guard looked at Larry's nose to nose and shouted back. "You are gonna be one if you don't get out of those damn boots." I know that Larry had never removed any boots so fast from his feet. Yes, he had approached a certain prisoner to get him a pair of those good boots from their supply room. He told Larry to leave $1.00 in that matchbox over near the drain and pointed it out and he would have the boots for him. This was sure a close call for Larry to come back home in Jackson.

I hope that by the time you have read this book this far, you realize a good steel erector must be housed in a good strong body, a body of bone and muscles ready to climb a bare steel column hundreds of feet into the air. Sometimes the column is waving in the air like a willow limb. He needs a specially developed body to withstand the heat and cold, plus many troublesome elements that God furnishes, such as strong winds, heavy rains and hail. I am convinced a man who survives the rugged life of a booming steel erector must have and maintain a well developed body of super flesh.

An unusual spirit built within the flesh of a man that enables him to do his daily work under these adverse conditions, must be present. This special desire for challenge and adventure is not found in all men. I have been astounded at how cool and calm men can be working eight hours or more each high day in the air and come down at nightfall so cool and composed. But I know that deeper within there is a big "thank you Lord" on their safe arrival on terra firma for all men do not make this safe return to the solid earth.

There is something special about the word *steel*. The sound of riveting guns, and large hammers beating the beams and columns to the proper place. The belch from the large crane drawing steel trusses high into the clouds. Watching the images of men perched atop the waving columns waiting for the beams arrival. The rugged pusher with a cob pipe filled with unbearable strong tobacco looking at a roll of blueprints for the entire complex. Checking each piece of steel as it goes up, as for holes, up side down, right end right. Looks as he would whip bears and wrestle alligators while he had some times off from work. But under the tough hide and behind the loud rough hollowing you find a tender soft heart that holds a compassion for every employee's family. Even the punks small daughter that had just stubbled her toe nail the night before. A thrill in his heart to see the complete gang go home happy and healthy at night time. And under his breath he says "Thank you God for another good safe day."

It's a thrill when the last piece of steel has gone up and been put in its proper place with the large American flag waving from atop. You see the business agents shaking hands with the happy customer commending each other on a good job well done. This is the big pay day.

They thank the workmen for their special efforts and pointing out on the road map the best way to get to the next job maybe in Oklahoma City or Gary, Indiana.

"See you there in work clothes Monday morning. Be sure and pack a big lunch."

Because the work is hard and the day is long.